A Field Guide to

NATIVE TREES & PLANTS of EAST END, ST. JOHN

U.S. Virgin Islands

MW01658262

A Field Guide to

NATIVE TREES & PLANTS of EAST END, ST. JOHN

U.S. Virgin Islands

by

ELEANOR GIBNEY

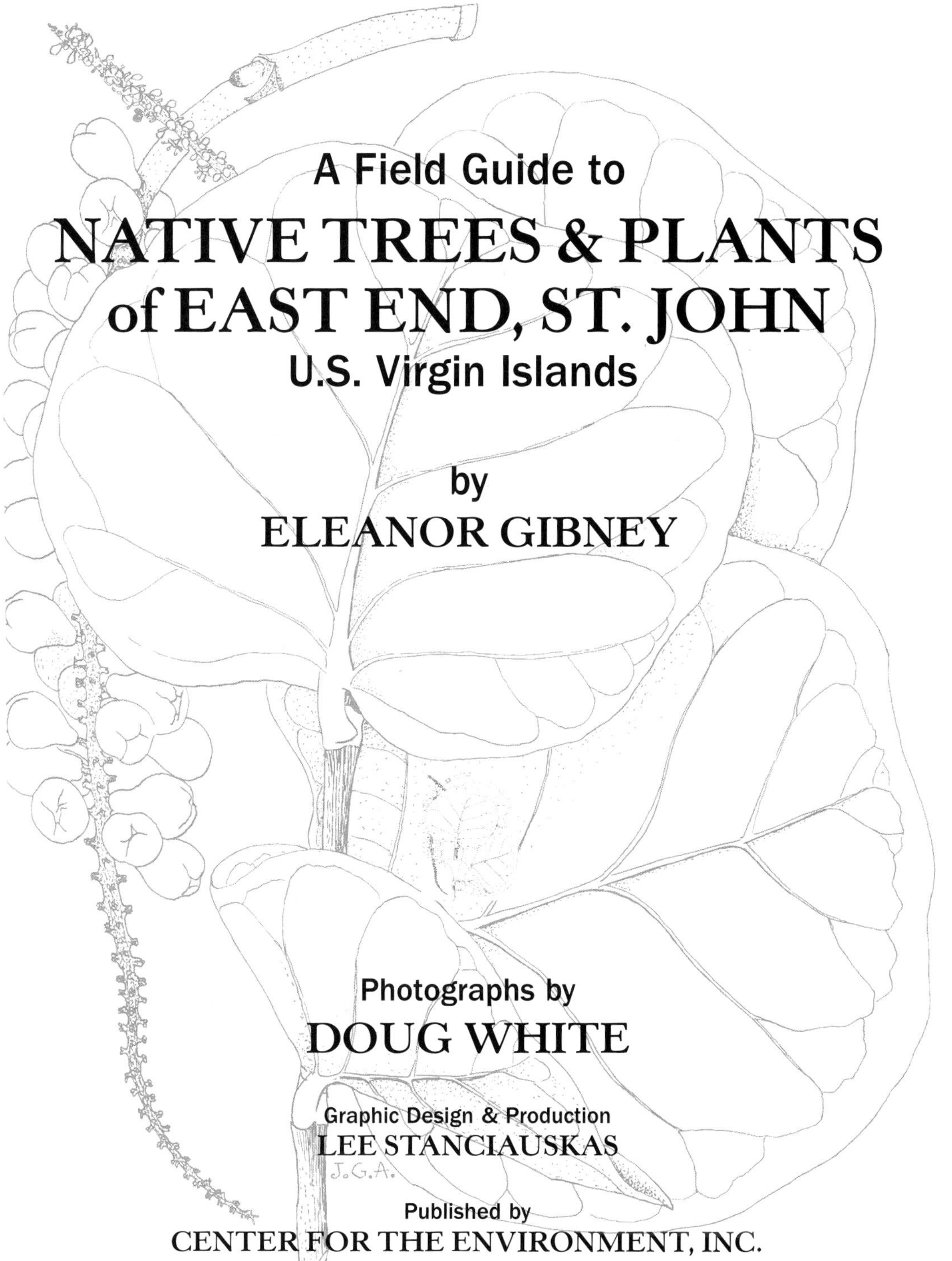

Photographs by

DOUG WHITE

Graphic Design & Production

LEE STANCIAUSKAS

Published by

CENTER FOR THE ENVIRONMENT, INC.

6Y-7 Hansen Bay

East End, St. John, U.S. Virgin Islands 00830

Copyright © 2004, by Eleanor Gibney

Photographs © by Doug White

Illustrations reprinted from *Common Trees of Puerto Rico and the Virgin Islands,* Elbert L. Little, Jr. and Frank H. Wadsworth, U.S. Department of Agriculture, Forest Service, Washington, D.C, July 1964 and *Trees of Puerto Rico and the Virgin Islands,* Second Volume, Elbert L. Little, Jr., Roy O. Woodbury, and Frank H. Wadsworth, U.S. Department of Agriculture, Forest Service, Washington, D.C, September 1974.

ALL RIGHTS RESERVED.
No part of this book may be transmitted in any form
by any means without permission in writing from the publisher.

Printed in the United States of America

First printing, 2004

ISBN: 0-9744795-0-0

Printed on 20% Kenaf "tree-free"/30% PCW (post consumer waste) recycled blend paper with soy inks.
All photography is digital, producing no chemical processing wastes.

Published by:
Center for the Environment, Inc.
6Y-7 Hansen Bay, East End
St. John, U.S. Virgin Islands 00830

This book was published for homeowners, builders and other residents of East End.
East End's awesome beauty and the environment are inseparably linked. If we preserve the environment, we preserve the beauty. If we destroy the environment, we destroy the beauty. The choice is ours!

ACKNOWLEDGMENTS:

The Publisher wishes to acknowledge that this book was make possible, in part, by Federal Funds. We thank the Urban and Community Forestry Assistance Program of the USDA Forest Service and the U. S. Virgin Islands Department of Agriculture for providing financial support for publication.

The Center for the Environment, a proactive environmental education non-profit, thanks the author for her tireless work and a lifetime of knowledge contributed to this publication without any financial remuneration whatsoever. The other primary participants, Doug White and Lee Stanciauskas, also donated countless hours, for which we are most grateful.

The photographer wishes to thank his wife, Leslie White, "chief spotter" who located many of the blooming trees and plants seen in this publication in the "bush."

Cover Photo: Ancient West Indian boxwood, Round Bay beach, East End
Back Cover Photo: *Oplonia Microphylla*

Introduction

This book is intended mainly as a guide to some of the more distinctive native plants seen on the East End of St. John, and in other arid parts of the Virgin Islands. We have not attempted to include all of the several hundred species found on the East End, but hope we have covered the most representative and interesting.

Through fortuitous accidents of geography and history, the island of St. John contains some of the most diverse remaining tropical dry forest in the Caribbean. Most of the island was cleared at one point or another during the Danish colonial era from 1717–1916, but apparently at least 50% of the island remained in forest or native shrub lands at any given time. So, when agriculture was abandoned on a particular property, there were usually plenty of native plants nearby to re-colonize the land. Of the 748 native or naturalized plant species growing "wild" on St. John, 643 are indigenous to the island, naturally occurring before the arrival of people.

The far end of St. John, east of Haulover Bay, is historically and geographically a very separate place with a unique history. As one of the most isolated and independent communities in the Virgin Islands, the East End settlement was successful due to the fortitude, cooperation and great resilience of the people.

Over the past 300 years the people of East End did significantly alter the natural environment, especially through goat grazing on the Round Bay side of the peninsula, but the prevailing dryness and windiness never allowed large-scale or commercial agriculture as it was practiced in the moister sections of the island. As a result, East End, along with the driest parts of the south shore, retains a remarkable diversity of native plants in several different habitats. The Privateer Bay area, in particular, contained almost pristine vegetation prior to the 1990's. This vegetation is composed primarily of hard-wooded trees and shrubs with extremely slow growth, requiring at least a century to attain to any significant size.

Thin crust of mosses, lichens and algae.

There are now two major threats to the cultural and natural landscapes of East End. The more obvious is the recent boom in "up-scale" residential development, including the large subdivisions at Haulover and Privateer. Perhaps even more damaging is the explosion of the feral goat population since 1990. Historically, goats were tethered or fenced on their owner's property, and any that roamed loose for long were hunted and eaten before they had a chance to reproduce in the wild. Now goat denudation of steep hills is causing a massive loss of soil, which certainly has a disastrous affect on the marine life in surrounding bays and limits any future recovery of diverse vegetation. Much of the damage goats do is to a thin crust of mosses, lichens and algae that covers the bare soil in these extremely dry areas, protecting against erosion by both wind and rain. The sharp hooves of the goats break

Native vegetation, Privateer Bay.

up this crust, it quickly disappears anywhere the goats walk frequently; the next heavy rain carries the thin soil quickly to the sea.

Along with a trend to construction of larger houses, far greater "earth change" and resulting environmental damage on residential building lots, there is a steady increase in imported landscape in the Virgin Islands. Garden plants originating in the far reaches of the tropical world are shipped in from Florida nurseries and "installed" along with the necessary drip irrigation systems. This is so much the way it is done now (by those who can afford it, anyway) that any other approach is seen as aberrant. In many cases it does appear to be the only option, since construction has obliterated most or all of the vegetation on the lot, and the owners have been assured by their contractor that this was worthless bush anyway. Beautiful native trees, many of them well over a century old, are destroyed daily on St. John. Granted, the beauty of many of these plants is a subtle beauty, one that takes a bit of consciousness to appreciate, and a bit of knowledge. For the most part, we scarcely see a plant if we do not know what it is (and it doesn't have a large red flower to shout, "look at me!"). Appreciation of these plants is appreciation of an intrinsic part of St. John, and a pretty big part, too.

This is not to say that non-native plants are necessarily bad. We are fortunate here that our periodic droughts and deluging rains are too extreme for most non-natives to move out of cultivation and take over native habitat, with some conspicuous exceptions. What is bad, very bad, is the plethora of insects and diseases that are brought in from Florida on the containers with the plants—with almost no agriculture left in the territory, there is no economic incentive to protect our gardens and forests. The number of serious plant pests in the territory has at least doubled in the past ten years, and there are probably less visible invaders such as microorganisms in the soils that may cause future problems.

It is our hope that this book will help preserve worthy plants in their habitats, encourage local propagation of the more useful and attractive, and help anyone so inclined to become greatly more connected to their surroundings—and enjoy them much more as a result.

TREES

Acacia macracantha / Acacia tortuosa

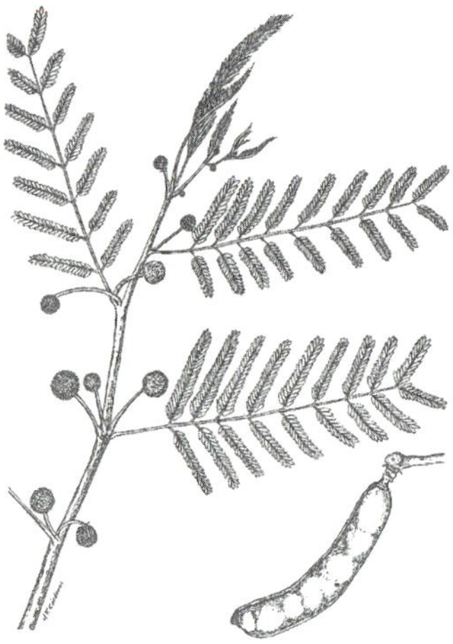

A. macracantha in bloom

Scientific name: *A. macracantha*

Common name: Stink casha, casha

Family name: Fabaceae, subfamily Mimosoideae (Mimosa subfamily).

Growth Form: Small spreading deciduous tree (*A. macracantha*); medium to large deciduous shrub (*A. tortuosa*).

Range: Bahamas to Barbados and northern South America (*A. macracantha*); Jamaica to Martinique and northern South America (*A. tortuosa*).

Leaf: Twice pinnate, pinnae 8–18 pairs (*A. macracantha*), 2–6 pairs (*A. tortuosa*); leaflets 8–18 pairs per pinnae, tiny.

Flower: Bright yellow globose heads, ¼ to almost ½ inch in diameter, composed of tiny flowers with numerous long stamens.

Fruit: Pods; in *A. macracantha* usually 3–5 inches long, ½ inch wide, flattened on the sides; in *A. tortuosa*—usually 4–7 inches long and ¼ inch wide, cylindrical.

Stem/Bark: *A. macracantha* generally single-trunked, with gray bark smooth or cracked, branches armed with long slender brown spines in pairs; *A. tortuosa* many-stemmed from the base, bark brown, paired spines grayish and conspicuous.

A. macracantha in bloom (detail).

COMMENTS:

These two species are lumped together here due to their great similarity. Both species are native to the drier areas of the region, but were probably much less common in the original vegetation. Grazing livestock will not consume casha plants because of the vicious spines, but will happily feed on the pods, distributing the small hard seeds (along with a pile of fertilizer) far and wide. In the V.I., land that has been heavily grazed quickly becomes dominated by casha and a few other

†*A. tortuosa in seed.*

spiny and/or toxic species that the animals shun. The stout long spines of both species apparently contain toxins that cause extra pain and swelling when embedded in skin.

On St. John *Acacia macracantha* has much the wider distribution, found in all but the moistest areas; *Acacia tortuosa* is confined to East End and a few pockets on the south shore.

Medicinal/Economic Uses: The hard wood has been favored for charcoal in the V.I. and was used for posts and construction in the past. *A. macracantha* has been used medicinally for treatment of fevers, chronic diarrhea, gangrene, skin infections, weakness and other maladies.

Landscape Uses: The long sharp spines may make them undesirable in many locations, but both species are interesting in appearance and the flowers have wonderful aromas. *A. tortuosa* can be trimmed to make a formidable hedge, useful for keeping humans out, and at least discouraging goats and donkeys.

Propagation: By the small hard seeds, which benefit from a soak in very hot water before planting.

Growth Rate: Moderate to fast.

Drought Tolerance: Excellent.

Wind Tolerance: Very good.

Salt Tolerance: Good.

Conservation Status: Not threatened.

A. macracantha in seed

A. tortuosa

Acacia muricata

Scientific name: *Acacia muricata*

Common name: Amarat, spineless acacia.

Family: Fabaceae, sub-family Mimosoidae.

Growth form: Shrub to small tree in East End and other very dry areas, medium tree elsewhere.

Range: Hispanola to Martinique

Leaf: Twice-pinnate, usually 3–5 inches long, secondary pinnae 3–6 pairs, leaflets usually 10–14 pairs per pinna; dark green above, whitish beneath; somewhat leathery, rounded at the tips. There is a very small cup-shaped gland between each pair of pinnae on the main leaf-stem.

Flower: Cylindrical spikes, 3 to 6 inches long, of many cream-colored flowers with minute petals and ¼ inch long thread-like stamens. Flowering intermittently, generally in spring or early summer.

Fruit: Dark brown pod, 3 to 5 inches long; flat, hard, slightly curved. Seeds 6 to 12, flat, thin, dark brown, about ½ inch long.

Trunk/Bark: Bark light to dark gray; forming rectangular plates in dry conditions such as East End, smoother elsewhere. Twigs spineless, cylindrical, with tiny brownish hairs when young; becoming smooth with raised white bumps (lenticles).

COMMENTS:

This wonderful native tree is very frequently confused with the aggressively weedy wild tamarind or tan-tan (*Leucaena leucocephala*). There is a strong superficial resemblance, particularly in the size and shape of leaves and pods, but amarat is an aristocratic hardwood, probably one of the cornerstone species of the original Virgin Islands forests. On East End and much of the south shore this is a shrub that dominates the less historically disturbed areas, rarely reaching more than 8 ft. on windy slopes, but to 20 ft. or more in sheltered guts and on leeward hills. In moist upland sections of St. John, it may appear to be a completely different species, soaring to heights of 50 ft., with a smooth straight trunk. Amarat leaves are excellent soil builders, creating a layer of soft duff that contrasts strongly with the hard and rocky substrate so commonly found.

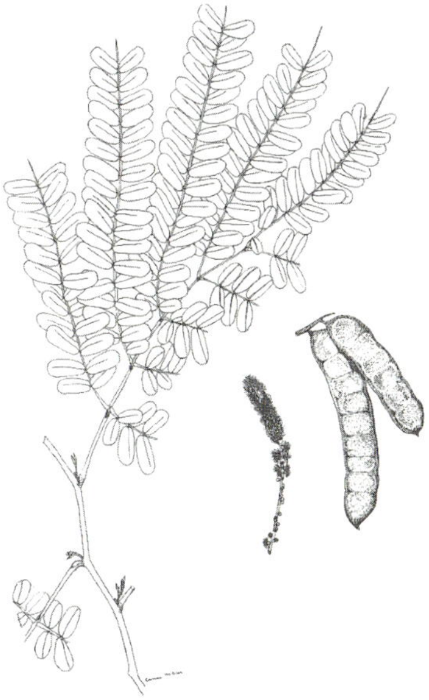

Medicinal/Economic Uses: Amarat was historically a prized building wood, especially useful for posts and footings that were buried or in direct contact with the ground. The handsome heavy wood is resistant to both rot and termites. Larger and straighter trees were probably systematically cut until the mid-20th century, so there may be no trees of optimal size presently seen in the region. Smaller trees were also much cut for charcoal production; one of St. John's few economic activities of the first half of the 20th century.

Propagation Methods: Seeds, with variable results. Germination is usually excellent, but subsequent growth may be slow and many seedlings die in the first year of life. This may be corrected to a degree by incorporating some quantity of soil from the base of the parent trees into the nursery mix. There may be very specific relationships with fungi and bacteria that are required for growth of the seedlings.

Landscape Uses: Ornamental shrub or tree; soil builder.

Growth Rate: Slow in normal East End conditions, moderate with additional moisture.

Drought Tolerance: Excellent.

Wind Tolerance: Very good.

Salt Tolerance: Moderate.

Conservation Needs: Amarat is common in the northern Virgin Islands, probably more so here than elsewhere in its limited range. While it will return to disturbed areas if they are somewhat moist, it does not compete well with weed species. The presence of abundant amarat in dry areas is usually an indication of relatively pristine vegetation. Many locally rare and endangered plants are found in association with amarat.

Adelia ricinella

Scientific name: *Adelia ricinella*

Common name: Adelia.

Plant family: Euphorbiaceae (Poinsettia family).

Growth form: Small spiny tree.

Range: Greater Antilles to Venezuela.

Leaf: Alternate, often crowded on twigs, thin, elliptic or obovate, ¾ to 1¼ inches long and ½ to ¾ inches broad.

Flower: Small, green, male and female on separate trees, male flowers short stemmed, female on stalks ¾ to 2 inches long.

Fruit: A three-lobed rounded capsule, about ¼ inches long, green or brown, containing three round gray seeds.

Stem/bark: Bark light gray, fairly smooth; twigs very light gray, often ending in a sharp spine approximately ½ inch long.

COMMENTS:

Adelia is a fairly common tree in all dry forests of the Virgin Islands. It is probably toxic to livestock, like most members of the Euphorbia family, and thus becoming commoner on East End as free-ranging goats continue to multiply. There is strangely little information on this species, with no common names or medicinal uses reported.

Medicinal/economic uses: Not known.

Landscape use: Resilient small tree for problem areas. Could probably be trimmed into a goat-proof hedge with little effort.

Propagation: By seed.

Growth rate: Slow to moderate.

Drought tolerance: Exceptional.

Wind tolerance: Good.

Salt tolerance: Fair.

Amyris elemifera

Scientific name: *Amyris elemifera*

Common names: Torchwood, candlewood, sea amyris.

Plant family: Rutaceae (Citrus family).

Growth form: Small evergreen tree.

Range: South Florida to Grenada, and mainland of Central America.

Leaf: More-or-less opposite, about three inches long; compound, with usually three, sometimes five, leaflets one to two inches long; with a strong aroma when crushed.

Flower: Small, to less than ¼ inch across; whitish, four-parted, in small clusters.

Fruit: Black berries, about ¼ inch in diameter, with a thin layer of flesh around the round brown seed.

Bark/stem: Bark gray, smooth on young trees, becoming rough and somewhat furrowed on older specimens.

Comments:

As the common names indicate, the wood of this handsome small tree has been used for torches in the past. The wood contains a quantity of flammable fragrant resin and reportedly will even burn when green.

The wood is also very attractive, very hard and very heavy (specific gravity 1.0–1.1). Perhaps due to the resin content, it is reported to be repellant to termites.

Larger trees were no doubt lumbered out of the region long ago, and due to the extremely slow growth of mature trees, we may not see any today at the potential size. The very closely related *Amyris diatrypa* is distinguishable by its leaves with prominent yellowish veins and stronger, slightly skunky, aroma; locally the two species are not differentiated by most people, due to their great similarity.

Medicinal/economic uses: The roots have been used as a hangover cure and an expectorant, the resin for the treatment of wounds and as a general tonic. Along with the uses of the wood noted above, it is also a favored charcoal species.

Landscape uses: Handsome small tree, excellent for screening due to the dense canopy of evergreen leaves.

Propagation: By seeds. **Growth rate:** Slow.

Drought tolerance: Excellent. **Wind tolerance:** Fair. **Salt tolerance:** Moderate.

Conservation status: Not threatened. There are reports of goats killing trees—by stripping off the bark—in extremely dry places such as Mona Island, west of Puerto Rico.

Bourreria succulenta

Scientific name: *Bourreria succulenta*

Common names: Pigeonberry, chink.

Plant family: Boraginaceae (Borage family).

Growth form: Small tree, more-or-less evergreen (often less in East End).

Range: Cuba to Venezuela.

Leaf: Alternate, elliptic; 1–5 inches long, 1– 2½ inches across; usually somewhat stiff, often hairy beneath.

Flower: White, fragrant, tubular with five spreading lobes, about ½ to ¾ inch across, in clusters typically 3–6 inches across. Blooming sporadically throughout the year.

Fruit: Nearly spherical, orange-red, about ½ inch across, containing four brownish, ridged seeds.

Stem/bark: Gray, smooth, sometimes becoming slightly corky. The trunk often has a sinewy or fluted appearance.

COMMENTS:

This is one of the commonest trees of dry forests in the Virgin Islands. The almost continual flowering and fruiting are surely important to many native insects and animals. The sweet smelling flowers are recorded to be abundant nectar producers, and as the common name implies, pigeons and many other local birds consume the fruit.

Economic/medicinal uses: The bark has been used to treat inflammation; the leaves are reputed to be aphrodisiac, although toxic to some livestock. The wood is reported to be hard and handsome, but little used due to small size of trees.

Propagation: By seeds. Seedlings and saplings do best with abundant sunlight.

Landscape use: Good small tree for open areas. The fragrant blooms and bright fruit clusters make this both ornamental and a good wildlife attractant. Goats apparently do not eat this tree.

Growth rate: Moderate to fast.

Drought tolerance: Excellent.

Wind tolerance: Fair.

Salt tolerance: Good.

Conservation status:
Not threatened.

Bursera simaruba

Scientific name: *Bursera simaruba*

Common names: Turpentine, gumbo limbo.

Plant family: Burseraceae (Frankincense family).

Growth form: Medium to large deciduous tree.

Range: South Florida, the Caribbean, and from Mexico to Northern South America.

Leaf: Alternate; pinnately compound, 4–8 inches long, with an uneven number of elliptic leaflets 1½–3 inches long; aromatic when crushed.

Flower: White, tiny, in small clusters. Blooming in spring. Male and female on separate trees (dioecious).

Fruit: In clusters; fleshy, reddish, diamond shaped and three-angled; about ½ inch long and ¼ inch wide, each containing one three-angled pink, white, or light brown seed. Fruits grow to almost full size within days of pollination, but remain on the tree for almost a year before fully ripening.

Bark/stem: Very distinctive, smooth red, red-brown or silvery; flaking and peeling to expose the greenish layers beneath.

Comments:

One of the most conspicuous trees of the Tropical American dry forest, turpentines are common enough to be ignored by most residents. The beautiful trunks, exemplary drought resistance, speedy growth and regional identity all recommend it, but it is very seldom planted locally.

The common names both refer to the aromatic gummy resin of the trunk. The aroma reveals the relationship to frankincense, a member of the same plant family. The uses of the resin are numerous (see below). The lightweight wood is not much used locally, but whole cut branches of the tree have been employed as "living fenceposts" by setting them, cut end down, in the ground at regular intervals and stringing wire from one to another. These branches would usually take root and grow, producing a more-or-less permanent and maintenance-free set of fenceposts. On St. John after Hurricane Marilyn, a large broken branch of turpentine that landed upright between two rocks was observed to root and put out new growth by the next summer.

Medicinal/economic uses: The resin has been used to treat many ailments, including back pain, impotence and fevers. Amerindians employed the resin as medicine, insect repellant, incense, glue, and canoe varnish and as a gum

smeared on branches to trap small birds. The leaves are made into a tonic tea, and the young leaves are reported to be edible when cooked. The wood has been used for many proposes elsewhere in the region.

Propagation: By the seeds, which mature and fall in late winter; or by cuttings of semi-hard to hard wood, best taken in the spring or early summer.

Growth rate: Very fast with water, moderate otherwise.

Landscape uses: Specimen tree, best sited where the trunk is fully visible.

Drought tolerance: Exceptional.

Wind tolerance: Good.

Salt tolerance: Good.

Conservation status: Not threatened.

Capparis cynophallophora

Scientific name: *Capparis cynophallophora*

Common names: Black caper, Jamaica caper, black willow.

Plant family: Capparaceae (Caper family).

Growth form: Small evergreen tree.

Range: Florida, Caribbean and Central America.

Leaf: Alternate, 2–4 inches long by ½ to 1½ inches wide, long—elliptic, somewhat thickened, usually dark green and shiny above, the lower surface covered with tiny golden scales. Note: juvenile leaves are very different in shape: linear, up to 10 inches long and only ¼ inch wide, not shiny, often almost black in color. These are generally seen on seedlings up to 3 feet, but injury to a mature tree may cause shoots with the juvenile leaf shape to sprout from the trunk or main branches.

Flower: Opening white, soon turning pinkish purple with age; with 4 petals about ½ inch long, and numerous spreading stamens about 2 inches long. Appearing throughout the year.

Fruit: A pendant brown pod, 4–7 inches long, with constrictions between the seeds; splitting open at maturity along one side to expose the bright orange-red interior and black seeds covered with thin orange-red pulp.

Bark/stem: Fairly smooth, light gray to black.

Comments:

The caper family is well represented with seven woody species on St. John. One of the most beautiful of regional trees, black caper has recently become extremely popular as a landscape tree in South Florida, where it is also native. This has led to the bizarre case of scores of black capers (or Jamaica capers as they are known in Florida) being shipped to the Virgin Islands from nurseries 1200 miles away. Unfortunately, these Florida plants are genetically quite distinct from our natives (e.g., they do not have a juvenile leaf form), but may breed with them, and thus alter the precisely evolved genetic abilities of our capers.

Locally, even experienced plant people may have a hard time differentiating between black caper and its close cousin white caper (*Capparis indica*). White caper differs in the leaves generally less shiny, more olive green than dark green, scales beneath leaves more silver than golden, and flowers that remain white rather than turn purple...otherwise the trees are extremely similar.

Incidentally, the black caper flowers open at night, and are very fragrant to attract pollinating moths. It is probable that the flower color changes to purple after pollination so as to be less visible at night—and not waste the attention of the moths.

Medicinal/economic uses: Teas and infusions of bark and roots have been used both externally for skin ailments and internally for hysteria, venereal diseases and worms. The pickled capers sold in small jars are the flower buds of the related Mediterranean species *Capparis spinosa*. Our native capers have similar but much stronger bitter flavor.

Propagation: By seed, collected when the pods are just splitting open.

Landscape use: Lovely small flowering tree, also suited for hedges, windbreaks and street planting. Once established, the tree will remain dark green and unruffled through the most severe droughts and hurricanes the region has to offer.

Growth rate: Moderate.

Drought tolerance: Exceptional.

Wind tolerance: Excellent.

Salt tolerance: Very good.

Conservation status: Not threatened in the northern Virgin Islands, very rare on St. Croix. Trees should be propagated locally and importation or unadapted genetic material from Florida should be avoided.

Cassine xylocarpa

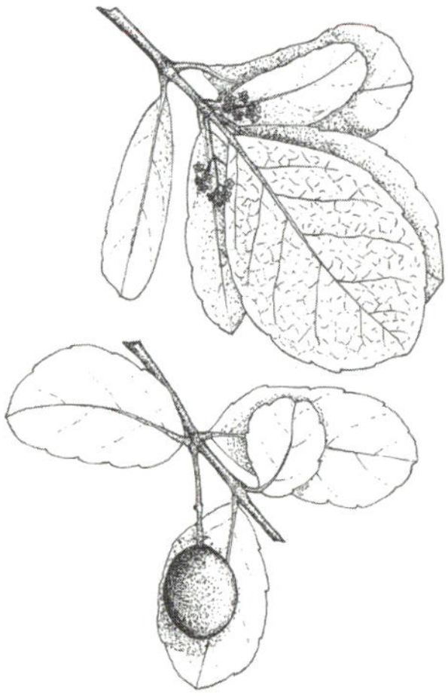

Scientific name: *Cassine xylocarpa*

Common names: Nothing nut, false nutmeg, marble tree.

Plant family: Celastraceae (Bittersweet family).

Growth form: Evergreen shrub or small tree.

Range: West Indies, Tropical American mainland from Mexico to Venezuela.

Leaf: Opposite, 1–4 inches × ¾ inch to 1½ inches, very stiff and leathery, ovate to rounded, variable at tip, often with small serrations on edge.

Flower: Tiny, greenish, in small clusters at end of branches.

Fruit: Rounded, yellow when ripe, about 1 inch across, containing one hard seed covered by thin flesh.

Stem/bark: Gray, fairly smooth, very often with conspicuous growths of bright orange smooth lichens.

COMMENTS:

All of the common names refer to the spherical woody fruits, which are generally regarded as useless, but these are a major component of the diet of native bats. This small tree or shrub is extremely common on all coastlines of the region, extending far inland only in very arid regions such as East End. The stiff leaves are impervious to salt and wind damage and are retained under the most rigorous droughts.

Medicinal/economic uses: The bitter thin rind of the fruit is reported to be edible, although certainly not especially palatable. The wood is hard, strong and attractive, but is little used locally, probably due to the small size of most trees.

Propagation: The hard fruits germinate fairly easily, although they may take several weeks.

Landscape uses: Excellent choice for windbreaks, screening and informal hedging, especially in front-line coastal situations.

Growth rate: Moderate, with water, otherwise slow.

Salt tolerance: Exceptional.

Wind tolerance: Excellent.

Drought tolerance: Excellent. Retains foliage under almost any conditions.

Conservation status: Not threatened.

Citharexylum fruticosum

Scientific name: *Citharexylum fruticosum*

Common name: Fiddlewood.

Plant family: Verbenaceae (Verbena family).

Growth form: Small to medium tree.

Range: South Florida and throughout the West Indies to Venezuela.

Leaf: Opposite, elliptic or oval, 2–4 inches long and 1–2 inches broad (larger elsewhere), stiff, frequently with orange stems, often turning entirely orange in drought conditions.

Flower: White, fragrant, about ¼ inch long, in drooping spikes 2–6 inches long.

Fruit: Oval, ¼ to ½ inches long, turning orange then black, containing four seeds. Reported to be edible but not too tasty.

Stem/bark: Bark very distinctive, light brown, shedding in long narrow strips.

Comments:

A common tree of both dry and moist forests, fiddlewood is found in all but the most arid sections of East End. The flowers are abundant nectar producers and birds are enthusiastic consumers of the fruit.

Medicinal/economic uses: Has been used to induce abortions and as a tea for respiratory problems. The wood is very hard and heavy (specific gravity 0.7); it has been used for cabinets, furniture—and musical instruments, as the common name implies.

Landscape use: Good tree for small gardens. The fragrant flowers and juicy fruits attract a variety of wildlife. The tree is unfortunately the host of a small leaf-tying caterpillar that can cause defoliation and messy leaf-drop once a year or so.

Propagation: By seeds, cuttings of semi-hard wood, or airlayers.

Growth rate: Moderate to fast.

Drought tolerance: Very good.

Wind tolerance: Fair.

Salt tolerance: Fair.

Conservation status: Not threatened.

Coccoloba uvifera

Scientific name: *Coccoloba uvifera*

Common names: Seagrape, grape tree.

Plant family: Polygonaceae (Buckwheat family).

Growth form: Spreading evergreen tree or shrub.

Range: Bermuda, Florida, the Bahamas and all shores of the Caribbean.

Leaf: Alternate, rounded; large, 3–7 inches long and 4–9 inches broad; stiff and leathery, mid-vein and larger side veins often red.

Flower: White, less than ¼ inches across, in spiky clusters to 10 inches long, male and female on separate trees.

Fruit: On female trees only, dark purple, about ¾ inch long, in pendant clusters, edible.

Stem/bark: Bark smooth, gray, often flaking off to expose brown under-bark

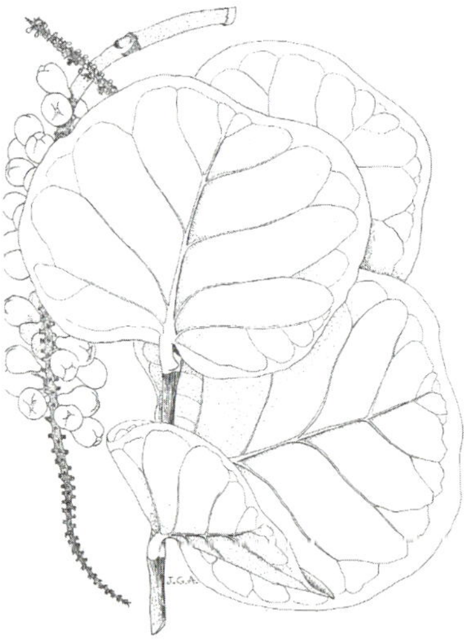

Comments:

Seagrape is one of the best known of native plants and one of the cornerstones of coastal ecosystems in the Caribbean. This amazingly tough species takes advantage of a niche, growing happily were few other plants can compete, tolerating salt and wind to an amazing degree. The importance of seagrape roots in stabilizing sandy

shores has often been dramatically illustrated locally, as sections of beach have almost disappeared following removal of the front line of trees.

On exposed rocky headlands seagrape can hug the rocks, forming a carpet or low hedge although many decades old, while in a moist back beach forest it can reach 45 feet.

Medicinal/economic uses: All parts of the plant have been used both internally and externally: in teas for chronic diarrhea, fever and internal bleeding and as a bath for rashes and sores. The astringent fruits are made into jelly and wine. The red wood is quite hard and has been used in fine woodworking.Unfortunately it is famously attractive to termites. The main recent economic use is as a landscape plant, with South Florida nurseries producing thousands of plants for shoreline planting.

Landscape use: Almost unrivaled for shorefront planting, especially on windy coasts. Useful for tall hedges and screening, slow growing on dry windy sites—in more protected areas it may become a large tree surprisingly fast.

Propagation: By cuttings, seeds or air layers. Sometime in the late 1990's a new pest appeared locally, probably arriving with seagrapes shipped from Florida: a shoot-boring grub that often kills or severely stunts young plants. Rooted cuttings appear somewhat more resistant to attack.

Growth rate: Slow to fast, depending on available moisture.

Drought tolerance: Excellent.

Wind tolerance: Exceptional.

Salt tolerance: Exceptional.

Conservation status: Not threatened.

Colubrina elliptica

Scientific name: *Colubrina elliptica*

Common names: Maubi, snakebark.

Plant family: Rhamnaceae (Buckthorn family).

Growth form: Shrub or small tree, at least partially deciduous.

Range: Florida to Venezuela.

Leaf: Alternate, thin and drooping, elliptic, about 1–2 inches long and ½–1 inch broad, light green.

Flower: Yellowish green, 5-parted, tiny, in small clusters at the leaf bases.

Fruit: A dry rounded capsule, about ¼ inch across, 3-seeded.

Bark/stem: Often multi-stemmed from base; bark brown or orange, splitting off or peeling in scales.

COMMENTS:

The name of this small tree is well known in the V.I. as the main ingredient of a fermented drink, called maubi or mabi, but probably few younger Virgin Islanders would recognize the tree, or find it in the dry forest. The very closely related shore maubi (*Colubrina arborescens*, see photos on this page) is common on nearby islands, but quite rare on St. John, where it is found around Hurricane Hole and Haulover Bay.

C. elliptica detail

Medicinal/economic uses: The very bitter bark, leaves, and roots have been used medicinally for treatment of fish poisoning (ciguetera), stomach ailments, syphilis and lung problems. The lightly fermented drink "maubi" is made from the bark combined with ginger and other herbs and flavorings. This drink is reported to have originally been a medicinal tonic, favored by the St. Thomas women who carried coal to refuel steamships in the days when Charlotte Amalie was a major re-coaling port. (It is not nearly as readily available as it once was, but still a feature of carnival food fairs. A bottled soft drink from Trinidad, "Maubi Fizz," is sometimes sold in local grocery stores. The wood is heavy (specific gravity 0.8) and hard, but too small for most uses.

Landscape use: An attractive ornamental shrub or small tree. The peeling bark is unusual, and the foliage has a somewhat grayish tone that looks right in a dryland garden or xeriscape.

Colubrina arborescens

Propagation: The hard shiny seeds can be germinated easily.

Growth rate: Relatively fast, especially for a hardwood.

Drought tolerance: Excellent.

Wind tolerance: Fair.

Salt tolerance: Fair.

Conservation status: Not threatened, probably less abundant than formerly due to careless collection of bark.

C. arborescens detail

Cordia ricksecekeri

Scientific name: *Cordia ricksecekeri*

Common names: Orange manjack, spruce almond.

Family name: Boraginaceae (Borage family).

Growth form: Medium-sized deciduous tree.

Range: Puerto Rico and the V.I.

Leaf: Alternate, ovate; relatively large, 4½–8 inches x 2–5 inches; upper surface rough-hairy, lower surface downy; very stiff and leathery. Totally deciduous in late winter.

Flower: Trumpet-shaped, orange to red-orange, about 1 inch long and ¾ inch across; blooming throughout the year, most abundant in late winter and spring.

Fruit: 1¼–1¾ inch long, conical, fleshy; light green, turning brown; seeds white.

Stem/bark: Light gray, rough.

Comments:

Orange manjack is a typical tree of dry coastal forests in the V.I. Its similar close cousin, *Cordia sebestena,* geiger tree, is often seen in cultivation here and perhaps is also native. Geiger is distinguished by the larger flowers, and larger fruit, which are white at maturity. Both species produce abundant colorful nectar-rich blooms that attract quantities of hummingbirds, especially in the dry late winter when little other nourishment is available.

Medicinal/economic uses: The hard wood of this species was used for charcoal production in East End (Kemp, 2002) and was probably used historically for cabinetry. The fruits are edible, although not especially palatable. Both this species and the similar geiger tree have been used to treat coughs, fever and intestinal complaints.

Propagation methods: Seeds, which germinate sporadically over 1 to 10 months, cuttings of semi-hard wood, or airlayering.

Landscape uses: Flowering tree, hummingbird attractant. **Growth rate:** Moderate to fast, with water.

Drought tolerance: Very good. **Wind tolerance:** Fair to good. **Salt tolerance:** Excellent.

Conservation status: Not currently threatened. Range is limited but habitat is abundant in range.

Eugenia biflora

Scientific name: *Eugenia biflora*

Common name: Rodwood.

Plant family: Myrtaceae (Myrtle family).

Growth form: Shrub to medium evergreen tree.

Range: Jamaica to Antigua and Mexico to Peru.

Leaf: Opposite, elliptic, ¾–2 inches long and ¼–1 inch wide, usually long pointed at tip, somewhat shiny, slightly stiff and thickened.

Flower: White, about ¼ inch long, with 4 very small petals and many spreading stamens; often very numerous for a short period in the spring or early summer following significant rainfall.

Fruit: Dark red at maturity, spherical or slightly flattened, about ¼–½ inch in diameter, containing one large seed.

Stem/bark: Bark light brown to gray, smoothish.

Comments:

One of the most widespread trees in Virgin Islands forests, this can be difficult to tell apart from several closely related trees and shrubs in the myrtle family. Among the myrtles with small and pointed leaves, this is the only one commonly found in dry areas—although it is not tolerant of highly exposed or windy sites on the East End. The fruit are sweet, with a slight resin flavor and are excellent in pies and preserves.

Medicinal/economic use: The stems of this and related Eugenias were favored for the braces of wire fish traps. The fruit have been consumed on a small scale.

Landscape use: Attractive slender evergreen tree or shrub, can be shaped as a hedge or less formal screen.

Drought tolerance: Good.

Wind tolerance: Fair.

Salt tolerance: Poor to fair.

Conservation status: Not threatened.

Exostema caribaeum

Scientific name: *Exostema caribaeum*

Common names: Princewood, yellow-torch.

Plant family: Rubiaceae (Coffee family).

Growth form: Small tree, semi-evergreen.

Range: South Florida to Grenada and Mexico to Costa Rica.

Leaf: Opposite, thin, elliptic, 1–3 inches long and ½–1¼ inches broad, with a tiny sharp point at the tip.

Flower: White, turning cream or yellowish with age, about 2½ inches long, with five very slender long spreading lobes, fragrant.

Fruit: A dry capsule, brown, elliptic, about ½ inch long.

Stem/bark: Bark dark gray; twigs slender, with each node bearing a pair of tiny bristle-like scales (stipules) that form a ring around the node.

COMMENTS:

The wonderful subtle fragrance of princewood flowers is unmistakable once one knows it. This little hardwood tree is common in coastal areas and appears fairly resilient to habitat disturbance. The flowers are actually among the largest in diameter of native plants, but the pale color and extreme narrowness of the petal-like lobes make them less than showy.

Medicinal/economic uses: The bitter bark has been used extensively as a substitute for quinine (the bark of a closely related South American tree), in treatment of malaria and other fevers. The yellow wood is very hard and dense (specific gravity 1.0) and burns easily. It has been used in fine woodwork and burnt for torches.

Landscape use: Attractive small tree; flowers with unusual form and great fragrance. Tolerates coastal conditions well, especially with a north or east exposure.

Propagation: By the small thin seeds within the capsules, also (with mixed results) by air layers.

Growth rate: Moderate, much faster with water.

Drought tolerance: Excellent **Wind tolerance:** Good. **Salt tolerance:** Very good.

Conservation status: Not threatened.

Ginoria rohrii

Scientific name: *Ginoria rohrii*

Common names: Water gregre, sugar ant.

Plant family: Lythraceae (Crape myrtle family).

Growth form: Small tree or shrub, deciduous.

Range: Hispanola, Puerto Rico and the Virgin Islands.

Leaf: Opposite, elliptic, 1–3 inches long and 1–2 inches wide, almost without stalks, with a reddish spot at the base of the mid-vein, shiny.

Flower: Appearing after spring rains, often when the plant is leafless; white, somewhat fluffy in appearance, about one inch across, in large clusters.

Fruit: Brown capsules, about ¼ inch long, containing many tiny seeds.

Stem/bark: Bark of mature trees light brown and divided into thick rectangular plates. Twigs with four short (but sharp) prickles at each node, two below each leaf.

COMMENTS:

One of the glories of the fleeting springtime that occurs in many years with the first hard rain after the late winter drought. In some springs the edges of ephemeral ponds—such as one across the road from the East End school house—are transformed by masses of fluffy white fragrant blooms. Writing about 1920, Nathaniel Lord Britton and Percy Wilson noted that engaged couples in the Virgin Islands might wait to set their wedding date until they were sure the ginoria would be in bloom to decorate the church.

Medicinal/economic uses: None known.

Landscape use: Beautiful seasonally blooming shrub or small tree, useful in borders or as a specimen. Tolerant of coastal conditions and salt marsh edges.

Propagation: By the small seeds or by air layering.

Growth rate: Medium

Drought tolerance: Excellent.

Salt tolerance: Excellent.

Wind tolerance: Good.

Conservation status: Not threatened.

Guaiacum officinale

Scientific name: *Guaiacum officinale*

Common name: Lignum vitae.

Plant family: Zygophyllaceae (Lignum vitae family).

Growth form: Small spreading tree.

Range: Throughout the West Indies, Panama and northern South America.

Leaf: Opposite, compound, with (usually) 4–6 leaflets, somewhat thickened, wedge-shaped, 1–2 inches long, often with orange veins and stems.

Flower: Blue, 5-petalled, almost 1 inch across, in showy clusters, mainly late winter to early spring but occasionally at other times.

Fruit: Flat capsules, orange at maturity, about three-quarters of an inch long, splitting open when ripe to reveal 1–2 dark brown seeds with a thin fleshy red covering.

Stem/bark: Light brown, peeling in scales to reveal green or gray smooth patches beneath.

COMMENTS:

Nearly extinct in the wild in the Virgin Islands, lignum vitae was probably once one of the commonest trees of East End and other arid areas. The tenacity, strength and beauty of this species make it a fitting symbol for the beleaguered dry forest of the region. A few trees are still present in the wild, and lignum vitae posts are visible on several old East End house sites. Many older trees in cultivation on St. John are descendants of the beautiful specimen near the post office in Cruz Bay. In recent years many have also been imported from Florida. Wild lignum

vitae is now rare or endangered through most of its original range. Trade of the wood is controlled under CITES (Convention on International Trade of Endangered Species) and locally the trees are protected by V.I. law.

Medicinal/economic uses: Lignum vitae was probably the most economically valuable tree native to the V.I. The resin content of the hard and heavy wood (specific gravity 1.3) is unique, making the wood self-lubricating; historic uses included bearings and blocks for the propeller shafts of steamships and bearings for roller mills. Less well-known are the medicinal uses. The resin and wood extracts were marketed in Europe beginning in the early 16th century as cures for a huge variety of ills, including syphilis; later the extract became "official" in medicine as a stimulant. Numerous local uses include treatments for rheumatism, gout, arteriolosclerosis, congestion, toothache, and skin fungus.

Landscape use: Beautiful small tree for gardens, street planting, etc. Growth is slow and full sun is required for good bloom. Buds open a rather dark blue and the flowers fade as they age, creating a lovely multi-toned display. The orange seed capsules are also very decorative.

Propagation: By the elliptic dark brown seeds. There is considerable variation in ease of germination from tree to tree and some seeds may take 6 months or more to sprout. Trees are very prone to root spiraling if kept in containers too long, this can lead to weak and easily blown over trees.

Growth rate: Slow. Responds well to water and fertilizer.

Drought tolerance: Exceptional.

Wind tolerance: Excellent.

Salt tolerance: Good.

Conservation status: Wild trees are very rare and locally protected in the V.I. Great care should be taken prior to land clearing on East End or the southeastern part of St. John (Coral Bay, John's Folly, etc.).

Gymnanthes lucida

Scientific name: *Gymnanthes lucida*

Common names: Crabwood, oysterwood.

Plant family: Euphorbiaceae (Poinsettia family).

Growth form: Small evergreen tree or shrub.

Range: Florida to Guadeloupe, and from the Yucatan to Honduras on the mainland.

Leaf: Alternate; dark green, often slightly shiny; stiff; 1½ to 3 inches long, ½ to 1 inch broad; generally elliptic, rounded or blunt at the tip; usually with some small teeth near the end that can be felt by running the finger along the edge.

Flower: Spike-like clusters of very tiny yellowish blooms, the spike one half to one inch long, the flowers slightly fragrant.

Fruit: About ⅜ of an inch across, rounded but somewhat three-lobed, usually containing three seeds; usually single on stalks 1–2 inches long; brown when mature.

Stem/bark: Dark gray or gray-brown, smooth or sometimes flaking on older trees.

Comments:

The sap of this attractive small tree is reported to be poisonous and cause skin rashes in some people, but this is apparently a rare occurrence. Like many of the dry forest species this is an extremely hard and heavy wood (specific gravity 1.1) and the wood has been used for small turned objects in the past.

Medicinal/economic uses: Reportedly used in Cuba as a medicine for "female problems" and elsewhere in the region the poisonous white sap (latex) has been used to remove warts and calluses by external application.

Propagation: By the seeds, which are easily removed from the ripe fruits. Gloves should be worn when handling green and sappy parts of the plant in case of sensitivity to the caustic latex.

Landscape uses: Small goat-proof specimen tree, also would be fine for screening or hedge. Grows best in shade.

Growth rate: Slow. **Drought tolerance:** Excellent. **Wind tolerance:** Good.

Salt tolerance: Good. **Conservation status:** Not threatened.

Krugiodendron ferreum

Scientific name: *Krugiodendron ferreum*

Common names: Ironwood, black ironwood, "ebony", ebonyberry, axmaster.

Plant family: Rhamnaceae (Buckthorn family).

Growth form: Small evergreen tree.

Range: South Florida, throughout the West Indies and South Mexico to Honduras.

Leaf: Opposite, about ¾ to 2 inches long by ½ to 1¼ inch wide, slightly notched at the tip, shiny, rather thin textured.

Flower: Tiny, yellow-green, 5-parted, in small clusters at the leaf bases.

Fruit: Black, rounded, ¼ to ½ inch long, containing one brown seed, edible.

Stem/bark: Light gray, fissured.

COMMENTS:

This common small tree grows in a variety of habitats in the V.I. Its handsome but unassuming appearance draws no attention to the fact that this is one of the world's hardest and heaviest woods (specific gravity 1.4). Its occurrence in South Florida makes it the heaviest wood native to the continental U.S.

Unlike some other local hardwoods, this was not driven to near extinction by historic exploitation, perhaps simply due to its prolific production of viable seeds and relatively quick growth. The local name "ebony" refers to the dark brown to black heartwood; the Belize name "axmaster" is certainly descriptive of the difficulty of cutting down a mature tree.

Medicinal/economic uses: The fruits are juicy and sweet, without much flavor yet pleasant. No medicinal uses are recorded in the Eastern Caribbean but the leaves are reportedly used as a tonic in Central America.

The wood is very durable and attractive but not much used locally, due to the small diameter of most trees.

Landscape use: Very nice small shade tree. The leafy canopy remains thick and green even in severe droughts.

Propagation: By the seeds, gathered when the fruit are dropping.

Growth rate: Moderate. **Drought tolerance:** Very good. **Wind tolerance:** Good.

Salt tolerance: Good. **Conservation status:** Not threatened.

Piscidia carthagenensis

Scientific name: *Piscidia carthagenensis*

Common names: Fish poison, Caribbean dogwood.

Plant family: Fabaceae, subfamily Faboideae (Pea family).

Growth form: Small deciduous tree to 45 feet, generally much shorter.

Range: Puerto Rico to the Lesser Antilles, and from Mexico to Peru.

Leaf: Compound, pinnate, consisting of 5–15 relatively large leaflets, these 3–7 inches long and 1½ to 4 inches wide, ovate, whitish on the lower surface, veins prominent; deciduous in late winter and spring.

Flower: In 3–10 inch long clusters; about ½ to ¾ inches across, whitish or pale pink, similar to pea flowers, abundant while the tree is leafless in spring.

Fruit: Distinctive light-weight winged pods, in conspicuous clusters, generally 2½ to 4 inches long, turning from bright green to brown before breaking into sections that are distributed by the wind.

Bark/stem: Light to medium gray, generally smooth or somewhat fissured.

COMMENTS:

This unassuming tree can be suddenly beautiful in flower or when covered with the ruffled lime-green pods. It is generally seen as a small, rather scraggly specimen, but can be an imposing tree in moister forests.

The tree has been prized for many uses in the past.

Medicinal/ economic uses: The bark or roots of this and other closely related species were used by the Tainos and Caribs to stupefy fish, which were then easily collected and consumed (this is now illegal in the territory). The narcotic properties have been well known in the region; decoctions have been used in the treatment of chronic pain, insomnia, and many other complaints. Nellis reports that the toxic compounds found in the roots of the very closely related *Piscidia piscipula* are numerous, including one which is lethal to fish at one part per million. The wood is hard and attractive and has been used for furniture. This is reported as one of the best charcoal woods, and Kemp and Benjamin list it among the traditional charcoal woods of East End. (We have no reports of the wood smoke having narcotic effects.)

Propagation methods: By seed or cuttings of young hard wood.

Landscape uses: Small flowering tree, also ornamental in fruit. Hummingbirds and other pollinators are attracted to the nectar-rich flowers.

Growth rate: Moderate.

Drought tolerance: Excellent.

Wind tolerance: Moderate.

Salt tolerance: Good.

Conservation status: Not threatened.

Pisonia subcordata

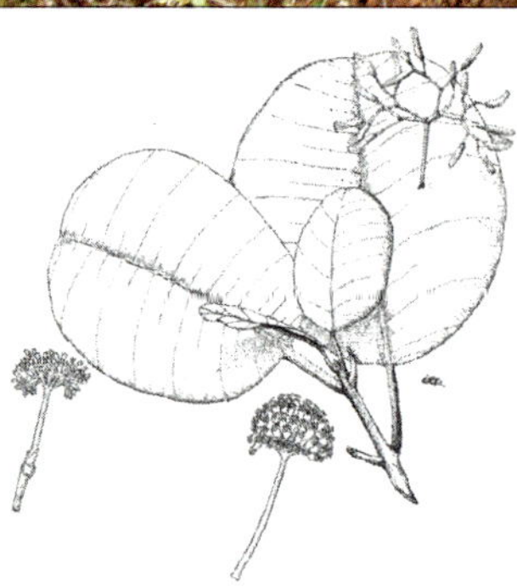

Scientific name: *Pisonia subcordata*

Common names: Water mampoo, loblolly.

Plant family: Nyctaginaceae (Four o'Clock family).

Growth form: Small to medium deciduous tree.

Range: Jamaica to Martinique.

Leaf: Opposite; relatively large, from 2½–6 inches long and almost as wide, occasionally even larger; rounded, with wavy edges.

Flower: Rounded, 1–2 inch wide clusters of small greenish blooms, fragrant. Generally blooming before the flush of new leaves, in late winter or spring. Male and female flowers are on separate trees (dioecious).

Fruit: Occurring only on female trees, a 2–3 inch cluster of half-inch long narrow blackish sticky seeds. The clusters fall off the tree in one piece and can form a messy layer under the tree.

Bark/stem: Bark distinctively smooth and light, trunks often rotund, with interesting exposed root systems.

COMMENTS:

Water mampoo is one of the most common and characteristic trees of the dry Eastern Caribbean forests. In contrast to the numerous species with hard and heavy woods found here, this is a soft wood that is considered generally worthless—this, combined with the relatively fast growth, may explain why there are many large water mampoos in the region. The size and the attractive exposed roots contribute to a very pleasing appearance.

Medicinal/economic uses: None known.

Propagation: By the sticky seeds, which are mature in late spring, or by cuttings of semi-hard wood.

Landscape uses: Specimen tree, shade tree. This is one of the few species capable of attaining significant size on very dry rocky sites. Female trees can be very untidy during the fruit-fall, so selection of cutting-grown male trees may be wise for planting close to houses. The sticky seed clusters may be only a mild annoyance to some; but others, especially owners of longhaired dogs, have found this to be a major nuisance for 2–3 weeks each year.

Growth rate: Fast.

Drought tolerance: Excellent.

Wind tolerance: Very good.

Salt tolerance: Excellent. May suffer from burning/die-back if subjected to frequent wind-born salt.

Conservation status: Not threatened.

Plumeria alba

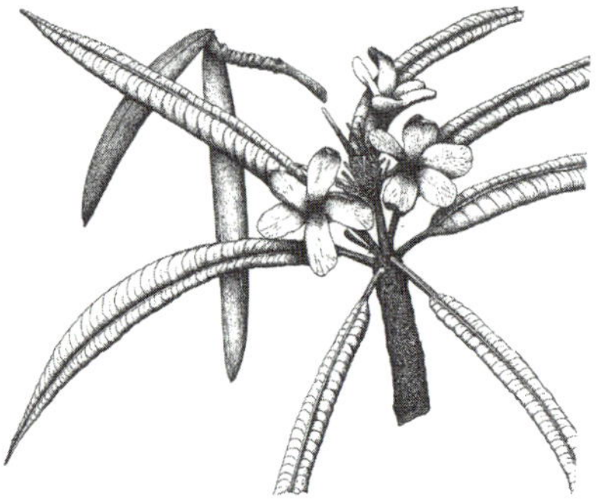

Scientific name: *Plumeria alba*

Common names: Wild frangipani, milk tree.

Family name: Apocynaceae (Dogbane family).

Growth form: Small tree.

Range: Puerto Rico to Grenada.

Leaf: Clustered at branch ends; very long and narrow, from 6–15 inches long and ½ –1½ inches wide; medium green and slightly shiny above, covered with tiny white hairs beneath, with edges turned under. Copious thick white sap (latex) will drip from any injury.

Flower: White with small yellow center, 5-petaled, about 2 inches wide, in clusters on stalks 3-6 inches long, extremely fragrant. Primarily April to October.

Fruit: Twin cylindrical pods, paired at the ends of old flower stalks, 4–6 inches long and about ¾ inch in diameter, pointed at ends. Pods split open at maturity, spreading to reveal numerous brown flat seeds with small papery wings on the edges.

Trunk/bark: Bark gray, smooth. Twigs cylindrical, somewhat succulent, yielding abundant white latex sap when injured. Latex is poisonous to ingest but generally causes no skin rashes. Wood surprisingly hard, heavy (specific gravity 0.8) suitable for cabinetry if trees are large.

Comments:

Wild frangipani is one of the most familiar and conspicuous plants of the Virgin Islands dry forest. The beautiful and fragrant blooms, and amazingly resilient nature of this species, should qualify it to replace the non-native ginger thomas (*Tecoma stans*) as the official territorial flower. Garden or broad-leaf frangipani, *Plumeria rubra*, is a close relative from the mainland of tropical America that is now widely cultivated throughout the warmer parts of the world.

The colorful caterpillar of a species of Pseudosphinx moth feeds exclusively on frangipanis, ingesting such quantities of the poisonous sap that they become toxic to birds or other predators. These caterpillars often defoliate trees, especially in the autumn.

Medicinal/economic uses: There are numerous medicinal uses described in the literature; almost all are extremely dangerous due to the poisonous nature of the entire plant.

Propagation methods: Both seeds and cuttings. Seedlings tend to produce a stronger root system. Collect seeds just as pods are splitting open—a plastic bag tied over the pod may save the wind-distributed seeds from being blown away. Cuttings should be woody, about 1-inch diameter and 10–12 inches long. Allow cut ends to dry for at least a few hours (several days would not hurt), root in well drained potting mix.

Landscape uses: Highly ornamental as a small specimen tree, particularly on very dry or rocky sites. Also extremely suitable for native re-vegetation projects, with high survival in harsh conditions. Due to the periodic defoliation by both caterpillars and fungus it is not recommended where a screen of foliage is desired.

Growth rate: Relatively fast with water and nutrients, moderate otherwise.

Drought tolerance: Exceptional.

Wind tolerance: Exceptional

Salt tolerance: Very good.

Conservation status: Due to great resistance to drought, hurricanes, and livestock grazing, and its copious seed production, wild frangipani remains common in all but the most disturbed areas of the Virgin Islands.

Reynosia guama

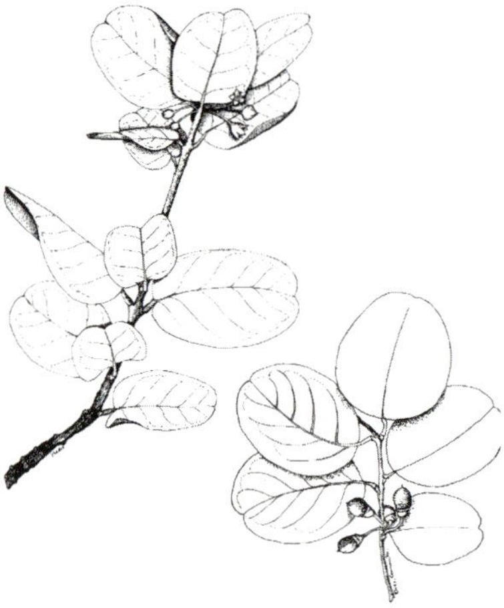

Scientific name: *Reynosia guama*

Common names: Guama, guamaberry.

Plant family: Rhamnaceae (Buckthorn family).

Growth form: Small evergreen tree.

Range: Puerto Rico and northern Virgin Islands.

Leaf: Opposite, elliptic to nearly round, about 1½–3 inches long and 1–2 inches broad, notched at the tip, thickened, dark green and shiny.

Flower: Tiny, yellow-green, several in small clusters at bases of leaves.

Fruit: Almost black when ripe, nearly ½ inch long, elliptic, with thin flesh and 1 large seed. Edible.

Stem/bark: Trunk slender, bark gray and fairly smooth.

COMMENTS:

Guama was known only from the northern Virgin Islands until the 1940s, when an overlooked population was discovered in the Guanica forest of Puerto Rico. It is fairly common in less-disturbed dry forests on St. John. The wood is hard, heavy and handsome, but of too small a size for practical use.

Medicinal/economic use: An alcoholic drink called guamaberry or warmerberry wine was made from the fruit soaked in rum with added spices. This was similar to the guavaberry rum that is still well known, but was apparently made only on St. John. The fruits are sweet and juicy but without any notable flavor.

Landscape use: Small tree with very attractive foliage.

Propagation: By seeds.

Growth rate: Slow.

Drought tolerance: Very good.

Wind tolerance: Good.

Salt tolerance: Fair.

Conservation status: Not threatened, should be preserved wherever possible due to very limited range.

Sideroxylon obovatum

Scientific name: *Sideroxylon obovatum*

Common names: West Indian boxwood, breakbill, pintop.

Plant family: Sapotaceae (Sapodilla family).

Growth form: Small to medium-large evergreen tree.

Range: Hispanola to Venezuela.

Leaf: Arranged in a spiral on the stem, wedge-shaped, usually ½–1½ inch long, very dark green, usually shiny, slightly thickened and quite stiff.

Flower: White, about ⅛ inch long, at leaf bases.

Fruit: Round, brown, about ¼ inch in diameter, containing one round brown seed.

Stem/bark: Brown and smooth on young trees and twigs, becoming gray and fissured.

Comments: These strong hardwood trees are seen at their largest and best on the East End shoreline, where apparently their shade and shelter were more valuable than their potential as fuel or construction material. Impervious to droughts and hurricanes, the magnificent specimens on Round Bay have survived for centuries. As with the large East Indian Tamarind trees, branches were cut for charcoal production, leaving the main trees intact. This is primarily a coastal tree, but it can grow high up on south-side slopes, including some near the summit of Bordeaux Mountain. Boxwood flowers may be produced at any time from late winter to early summer and have a peculiar pungent malty aroma, reminiscent of a brewery.

Medicinal/economic uses: None known, aside from charcoal and woodworking.

Landscape use: Excellent shade tree for exposed windy locations. Can also be trimmed for dense hedges and windbreaks.

Propagation: By seed.

Growth rate: Slow.

Drought tolerance: Exceptional

Wind tolerance: Exceptional.

Salt tolerance: Exceptional.

Conservation status: Not threatened.

Tabebuia heterophylla

Scientific name: *Tabebuia heterophylla*

Common names: White cedar, pink cedar.

Family name: Bignoniaceae (Trumpet-vine family).

Growth form: Shrub to 60 foot tree, depending on conditions.

Range: Hispanola through Lesser Antilles.

Leaf: Opposite; generally palmately compound, with from 1–5 elliptic leaflets. Extremely variable in size, color and shape (the species name, "heterophylla" means "different leaf"). East End plants tend to have smaller and fewer leaflets than those in moister areas.

Flower: Trumpet-shaped; pale pink, purple or almost white, with yellow throats; about 2 inches across and 2½ inches long, in clusters at branch ends. Primarily spring, but sporadic at other times.

Fruit: An almost cylindrical pod, 2½–5 inches long and ¼ inch broad; splitting open at maturity to reveal many close-packed thin seeds with whitish papery wings, about ½ inch long.

Stem/bark: Bark rough, gray, becoming furrowed with age.

Comments: White cedar is among the prettiest and most profusely blooming native trees, with a huge environmental tolerance. The shrubby specimens clinging to the rocks of East End and the south shore bear little resemblance to the straight tall trunks and deep green leaves seen on Bordeaux mountain, but we are assured these are the same species. The lovely flowers are a rich supply of nectar for hummingbirds and many other visitors. The common name comes from the quality of the strong, moderately heavy wood, which was highly regarded for boat building in the Eastern Caribbean. We probably see few trees at anything like their optimal size in the V. I., since all larger specimens would have been lumbered, up until at least the early 1960's. Tortola boat

builders reportedly imported cedar from eastern St. John, having exhausted their own supply. Many related *Tabebuias* from Central and South America are economically important timbers (ipe, primivera) or ornamentals (yellow poui, pink poui).

Medicinal /economic uses: The bark, leaves and other parts have been used as a tea for aches, pains and bed-wetting. This and other species of *Tabebuia* may contain promising antibiotic alkaloids. The wood has been used for all manner of construction and cabinetry.

Propagation methods: By the abundant winged seeds, which germinate readily, or by cuttings of semi-hard wood.

Landscape uses: Flowering tree or shrub, reforestation.

Growth rate: Medium.

Drought tolerance: Very good.

Wind tolerance: Excellent.

Salt tolerance: Excellent.

Conservation status: Not threatened.

SHRUBS

Crossopetalum rhacoma

Scientific name: *Crossopetalum rhacoma*

Common names:
Maidenberry, poison cherry.

Plant family:
Celastraceae (Bittersweet family).

Growth form: Woody evergreen shrub.

Range: South Florida to St. Lucia, Mexico to N. South America.

Leaf: Opposite, small (½–1½ inch long and ¼ to ¾ inch wide), with wavy edges, rounded or pointed at end.

Flower: Tiny, reddish, in clusters at the leaf bases.

Fruit: Bright red, oval to globose, about one-quarter inch long, containing a single brown seed.

Stem/bark: Gray, somewhat flaky, twigs very slender.

COMMENTS:

This common shrub is often overlooked, but it is very attractive in a modest way. The common name "poison cherry" is off-putting, but apparently without any basis: there are no reports of anything toxic associated with the plant.

Medicinal/economic uses: The whole plant, particularly the roots, has been used in treatment of kidney and urinary problems. The small berries are edible, although not too flavorful.

Propagation: By the seeds, which can easily be removed from the ripe fruit. Germination and seedling growth may be fairly slow.

Landscape uses: *Crossopetalum* is an excellent choice for borders and hedges. With pruning, the open growth can be made more compact and dense.

Growth rate: Slow to moderate.

Drought tolerance: Good.

Wind tolerance: Good.

Salt tolerance: Very good.

Conservation status: Not threatened.

Croton betulinus

Scientific name: *Croton betulinus*

Common names:
Pistarckle bush, broom bush.

Plant family:
Euphorbiaceae (Poinsettia family).

Growth form: Low shrub.

Range: Cuba to Grenada.

Leaf: Alternate, ¼–1 inch long and ¼–½ inch wide, margins with small rounded lobes, underside with dense short white hairs, not aromatic or only slightly so.

Flower: Whitish, 5-parted, in terminal spikes ½–1¼ inches long.

Fruit: A 3-lobed capsule, less than ¼ inches across.

Stem/bark:
Stems wiry, thin; bark dark brown.

Comments: Less common than its maran cousins *Croton flavens* and *Croton astroites,* this smaller shrub is quite different in appearance. The stiff yet flexible stems were made into brooms in the past. Pistarckle is a Dutch Creole word meaning "a big noise and commotion". It is not evident what connection that has with this modest plant. Like all crotons, this is poisonous.

Medicinal/economic uses: The brooms mentioned above.

Landscape use: A useful "filler" shrub, could be used as a soil stabilizer to revegetate roadsides, etc.

Propagation:
By seeds or cuttings.

Growth rate:
Moderate.

Drought tolerance:
Excellent.

Wind tolerance:
Good.

Salt tolerance:
Fair.

Conservation status:
Not threatened.

Croton flavens var. rigidus

Scientific name: *Croton flavens var. rigidus*

Common names:
Yellow maran, soldier whip.

Plant family:
Euphorbiaceae (Poinsettia family).

Growth form: Woody shrub.

Range: Species occurs throughout the West Indies and in northern South America, variety *rigidus* is found only in Puerto Rico and the Virgin Islands.

Leaf: Alternate, elliptic or oval, 1–3 inches long and ½ to 1 inch wide, very densely covered with short gray or yellow star-shaped hairs, with strong aroma when crushed.

Flower: Small, white, 5-parted, in terminal spikes 2–4 inches long.

Fruit: A capsule less than ¼ inch across, 3-lobed, 3-seeded.

Stem/bark: Twigs densely covered with yellow-white or yellow-brown short hairs.

Comments:

Familiarity does tend to breed contempt for this shrub, but its ubiquity is entirely human caused. Yellow maran is very toxic to livestock, quickly becoming dominant on land where all more palatable species have been consumed. Yellow maran and its close cousin white maran (*Croton astroites*) are now the main woody vegetation on many small cays and islands (particularly in the British Virgin Islands) where goats or sheep have been set loose. The present day explosion of feral goats on East End is quickly turning diverse native shrublands into blasted deserts of maran and thorn bushes.

White maran, which is also present on East End, differs from this species in the taller stems (to 10 ft. or more vs. generally under 6 ft.) and larger leaves with pointed tips, heart-shaped at the base, only slightly aromatic.

The wildly colorful garden "croton" is an Asian plant in the same family that was originally placed in the same genus, but was long ago re-classified as *Codiaeum variegatum.*

Medicinal/economic uses: This poisonous plant has been used as a remedy for venereal diseases. It is not at all recommended. The leaves were formerly used effectively for scrubbing pots.

Landscape use: Although this is not at all an unattractive plant, its charms are hard to appreciate due to its goat-induced proliferation. Could be quite useful as soil stabilizer on over-grazed slopes.

Propagation: By seeds or cuttings. **Growth rate:** Moderate to fast. **Drought tolerance:** Exceptional

Wind tolerance: Excellent. **Salt tolerance:** Very good.

Conservation status: Not threatened, to say the least.

Eugenia sessiliflora

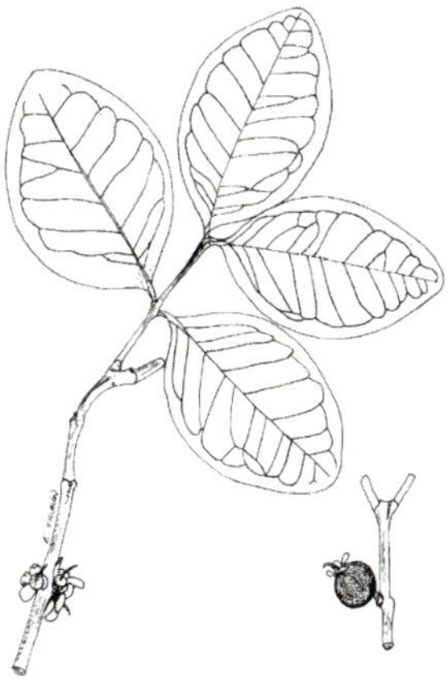

Scientific name: *Eugenia sessiliflora*

Common name: None known.

Plant family: Myrtaceae (Myrtle family).

Growth form: Woody evergreen multi-stemmed shrub or small tree.

Range: Puerto Rico and the Virgin Islands.

Leaf: Opposite, almost stemless, 2–3 by 1½–2½ inches, round or rounded-oval, very thick and rigid, margins turned under, dark green with prominent yellowish veins, pleasantly aromatic when crushed.

Flower: White, about a half inch across, with many projecting stamens; stemless, from the leaf bases or directly from the woody trunk. Generally blooming in spring or early summer.

Fruit: Round, red when ripe, about 1 inch across, often appearing on the woody trunk.

Bark/stem: Usually with many stems from the base; bark smooth and pale, whitish to gray; twigs reddish brown.

COMMENTS:

The genus Eugenia is well represented on St. John by 12 native trees and shrubs, all handsome, but *Eugenia sessiliflora* is a particularly wonderful plant. This extremely slow-growing shrub appears to not survive in areas of intense historical use, and thus is often an indicator of fairly pristine conditions, often found in association with very rare species. The rigid leaves are filled with aromatic oil, reminiscent of the related bayrum tree, or the more distantly related tea tree and eucalyptus of Australia. The north side of East End has many beautiful specimens that may be 100 to 200 hundred years old, or more.

Medicinal/economic uses: None reported. The aroma of the foliage suggests benefits to the sinuses and lungs when inhaled.

Landscape use: Beautiful dense shrub, suitable for hedges, if you are patient.

Growth rate: Slow.

Propagation: By the large seeds. Plants do not do well if left in pots for very long.

Drought tolerance: Excellent, especially if in a shaded position.

Wind tolerance: Excellent. **Salt tolerance:** Very good.

Conservation status: Not yet threatened, may become so in future due to limited range and slow growth. Should certainly be protected from needless destruction during surveys and construction.

Euphorbia petiolaris

Scientific name: *Euphorbia petiolaris*

Common names:
Hill manchineel, black manchineel.

Plant family:
Euphorbiaceae (Poinsettia family).

Growth form: Small deciduous tree.

Range: Easternmost Bahamas to Margarita (off coast of Venezuela).

Leaf: Whorled, 3–8 at the nodes; stems long and slender, ½–1½ inch long; leaf blades rounded, thin textured, about ½ inch long and broad, lighter green beneath.

Flower: Separate male and female flowers on the same plant, both very small, yellow-green, with 5 lobes.

Fruit: A dry capsule, 3-lobed, about ¼ inch long, containing 3 seeds.

Stem/bark: Bark very distinctive: smooth, shiny, dark brown, peeling off in thin papery layers, reminiscent of cherry bark. Cut stems exude copious poisonous white sap.

Comments:

An elegant small tree with a very bad reputation, perhaps not fully deserved. As the common names indicate, this relative of manchineel (*Hippomane manchinella*) has similar caustic sap; folk wisdom and literature both stress the dire consequences of exposure, but casual contact appears harmless. Plant researchers in the region have been unavoidably exposed while working in dry shrublands, with no ill effects. This is not to say the plant isn't poisonous—like all members of the Euphorbia family it should be treated with respect.

Medicinal/economic uses: The sap has been used to remove warts.

Landscape use: Since this is certainly no more toxic than several related species of *Euphorbia* that are commonly cultivated in the V.I., there is little reason to shun it, but do use caution in avoiding the sap. The handsome bark and delicate foliage make this a great addition in most landscapes.

Propagation: By seed.

Growth rate: Fast.

Drought tolerance: Excellent.

Wind tolerance: Fair.

Salt tolerance: Not known.

Conservation status: Not threatened.

Helicteres jamaicensis

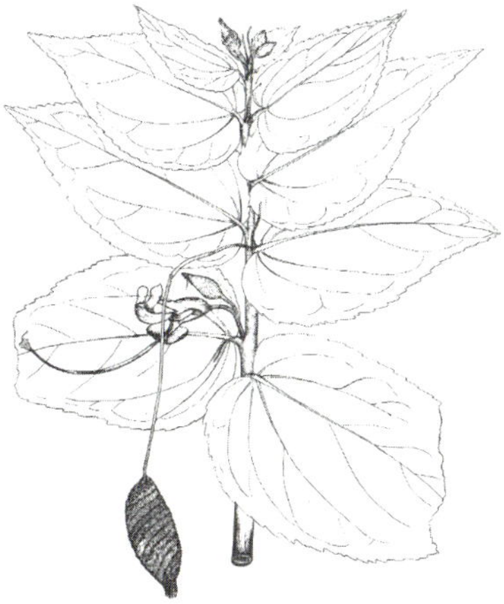

Scientific name: *Helicteres jamaicensis*

Common names: Cowbush, cat's balls.

Plant family:
Sterculiaceae (Chocolate family).

Growth form: Tall shrub.

Range: Bahamas to St. Martin.

Leaf: Alternate, not symmetrical, 3–7 inches long and 2–4 inches wide, densely soft hairy on both surfaces, edges coarsely and unevenly toothed.

Flower: White, irregular in shape, with 5 petals a bit more than 1 inch long and protruding column about 2½ to 3 inches long.

Fruit: Very unusual, spirally twisted, yellow-green to brown, covered with dense gray hairs, about 1½ to 2 inches long, hanging on a 3 inch stalk, containing many brown seeds.

Stem/bark: The bark is gray and bumpy.

COMMENTS:

This conspicuous shrub of very dry areas looks like a fast growing weed, but is actually a hard-wooded and fairly long-lived plant. The leaves are larger than any others in this plant community, protecting themselves from dehydration with thick wooly hair rather than by being small and leathery.

The twisted seedpods are noteworthy; common names elsewhere include "screw tree" and "cotton rat", both quite descriptive.

Medicinal/economic uses: A tea has been used to treat fevers, coughs and tuberculosis. A decoction of the root has been used in Jamaica to control hemorrhage.

Landscape use: Interesting shrub for the dry garden; the large soft leaves contrast strongly with typical drought resistant species.

Propagation: By seeds.

Growth rate: Fast.

Drought tolerance: Excellent.

Wind tolerance: Fair.

Salt tolerance: Fair.

Conservation status: Not threatened.

Heliotropium ternatum

Scientific name: *Heliotropium ternatum*

Common name: Cliff heliotrope.

Plant family:
Boraginaceae (Borage family).

Growth form:
Low evergreen shrub to 20 inches high, many-branched from base.

Range: West Indies and northern South America.

Leaf: Usually in whorls of three, generally ½ to one inch long and ⅛–¼ inch wide, thickened, strongly turned under at edges, often silvery in appearance due to whitish hairs. Slightly resembles rosemary.

Flower: White, tiny, in coiled 1–1½ inch long spikes at the branch tips.

Fruit: Tiny, rounded, dry, splitting into two seeds.

Stem/bark: Woody at base, with many spreading branches.

COMMENTS:

This low ground-covering shrub of dry areas is frequently a companion of the similarly formed old woman's broom (*Turnera diffusa*).

Both are characteristic of open arid lands that may have been grazed in the past, but not burned or otherwise drastically altered. Cliff heliotrope is apparently unpalatable to goats, and thus has survived well on the East End and drier parts of the south shore.

Medicinal / economic uses: None known; other (weedy) local heliotropes have many medicinal applications in the region.

Landscape use: The dense low growth, attractive silvery foliage and petite white flowers make this a very desirable ground cover.

Propagation: By cuttings of the woodier stems; or by the minute seeds (barely cover with very well drained potting soil). Does best in full sun.

Growth rate: Slow.

Drought tolerance: Exceptional.

Wind tolerance: Excellent.

Salt tolerance: Fair.

Conservation status: Not threatened; should be preserved wherever possible due to limited habitat and intolerance of major disturbance.

Jacquinea arborea / Jacquinea berterii

Jacquinea berterii

Scientific name: *Jacquinea berterii*

Common names: Jacquinea, little-leaf jacquinea, barbasco.

Plant family: Theophrastaceae (Theophrasta family)

Growth form: Woody evergreen shrub or small tree.

Range: Bahamas to Guadeloupe.

Leaf: Spiraled or whorled, usually 1–2 inches long and ¼–½ inches wide, very stiff, usually spoon-shaped, edges slightly turned under, almost stalkless.

Flower: White or yellowish, on down-curved stalks at the bases of the leaves, about ¼ inches long and wide, 5-parted, fragrant.

Fruit: Yellow or orange, rounded, pointed at the tip, ¼ inches across, containing one or more seeds, possibly poisonous.

Stem/bark: Bark dark gray to almost black, twigs brown.

COMMENTS:

One of most beautiful of native plants, the elegant jacquinea is blessedly unpalatable to livestock, and has thus survived except in areas that were repeatedly burned in the past. This is a very slow growing plant; larger specimens in very arid locations are estimated to be 200 or more years old. The appearance often suggests a natural bonsai or a Chinese painting, but this is very much a Eastern Caribbean native.

The very closely related large-leaf jacquinea (*Jacquinea arborea*) is similar, but with much larger leaves, which are strongly curved under at the edges; and upright flowers. It is generally found very close to the sea.

Jacquinea berterii berries

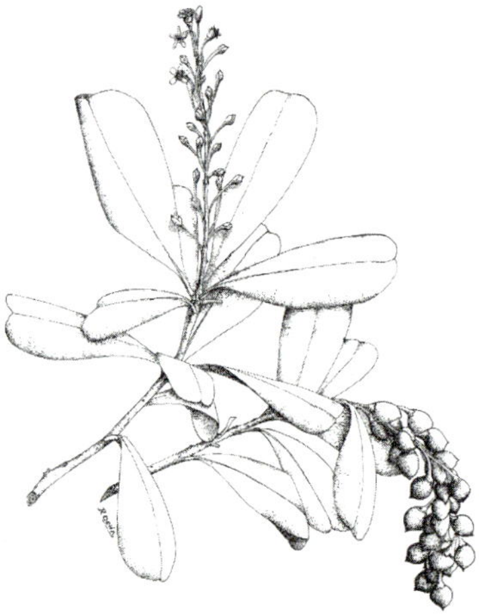

Jacquinea arborea

Jacquinea arborea in bud

Medicinal/economic uses: None known. The fruits of related species have been used as a fish-poison, and all jacquineas apparently contain a strong repellant against predatory insects. The wood burns well and this is one of many plants that may be called torch or torchwood, names we omit here due to potential confusion.

Landscape use: Highly ornamental shrub, can be a focal point in the landscape.

Should be preserved and protected whenever possible, due to very slow growth and difficulty of propagation. Naturally occurring plants are impervious to stress and virtually problem free.

Propagation: By seeds, which may be difficult to find and slow to germinate. Plants do not do well in pots and are not easily transplanted, so should be moved to their permanent location soon after germination.

Growth rate: Very slow.

Drought tolerance: Exceptional.

Wind tolerance: Exceptional

Salt tolerance: Very good.

Conservation status: Not yet threatened, but seedlings are rare, and mature plants are constantly destroyed through ignorant construction practices.

Lantana involucrata

Scientific name: *Lantana involucrata*

Common names: Sage, pink sage.

Plant family: Verbenaceae (Verbena family).

Growth form: Shrub, to 6 ft. tall, usually shorter.

Range: Florida, West Indies, Mexico to Venezuela.

Leaf: Opposite, ½–2 inches long, with short stiff hairs above and dense downy hairs beneath, margins with small rounded teeth; aromatic when crushed.

Flower: Lavender, small, in dense heads about 1 inch across.

Fruit: A small cluster of bright purple berries packed close together, the whole somewhat resembling a raspberry.

Stem/bark: Many branched from near the base, stems slightly 4-angled, smooth.

Comments:

While other local lantanas tend to be exclusively weedy, this agreeable shrub is often found in very undisturbed areas. It is poisonous to livestock, so it is certainly commoner where land has been grazed.

Related West Indian lantanas with orange or multicolored flowers are now weeds spread over the entire tropical world.

Medicinal/economic uses: This and other species of lantana have been used to treat a wide variety of ailments, taken as a tea or in aromatic bathes. The plant, especially the green fruits, is toxic and should be handled with caution. The leaves have been used as bait in fishtraps.

Landscape use: Flowering shrub for borders, hedges, soil stabilization and sea shore plantings. Tolerates sandy soil very well.

Propagation: Easy by cuttings or seed, growth is best in full sun.

Growth rate: Moderate to fast.

Drought tolerance: Excellent.

Wind tolerance: Very good.

Salt tolerance: Excellent.

Conservation status: Not threatened.

Machaonia woodburyana

Scientific name:
Machaonia woodburyana

Common name:
Woodbury's machaonia.

Plant family:
Rubiaceae (Coffee family).

Growth form: Woody shrub.

Range: St. John and Virgin Gorda.

Leaf: Opposite or appearing whorled; tiny, generally about ¼ inch long; usually rounded at the tip and tapered toward the base, thin textured, slightly shiny.

Flower: White, tiny, 4-lobed, in clusters at the ends of the branches.

Fruit: Dry, brown, flat and slightly diamond shaped, about ¼ inch long.

Stem/bark: Multi-stemmed from the base, the main branches with numerous short side branches and paired spines at nodes.

COMMENTS:

One of the rarest plants of the Virgin Islands, Woodbury's machaonia was first discovered in the early 1980's on East End by Roy Woodbury, a University of Puerto Rico botanist hired by V.I. National Park to conduct the first full inventory of St. John's flora. Woodbury's search lead to the discovery of two species new to science (of which this was one), and dozens that were not previously documented as occurring on St. John. Woodbury's machaonia is now a locally protected plant, and it appears that the world's largest population lies within the boundaries of the Privateer Bay subdivision on East End. The area had relatively little historical use, and this inconspicuous shrub was apparently never noted as different from somewhat similar species in the area. Unfortunately, the subdivision road construction at Privateer in the early 1990's destroyed a large number of the population, but covenants are in place to protect remaining plants. Several of the new landowners in the project have expressed an interest in helping preserve this unique piece of St. John's natural heritage. Two shrubs on the East End are often confused with *Machaonia*; see *Oplonia*, page. 53 and *Scolosanthus*, page 59.

Medicinal/economic uses: None known, the plant has apparently always been rare enough to escape notice.

Landscape use: Handsome shrub, would make excellent hedge if patience allowed for the slow growth. Natural occurrence is mainly on east or northeast facing slopes.

Propagation: By the dry seeds. Seedlings are very sensitive to overwatering, and should be protected from heavy rain until well established in the ground.

Growth rate: Very slow.

Drought tolerance: Excellent.

Wind tolerance: Good.

Salt tolerance: Not known, probably poor.

Conservation status: Highly threatened. Only significant population on U.S. soil is on East End, on private property. A small population on Virgin Gorda is also unprotected.

Melochia tomentosa

Scientific name: *Melochia tomentosa*

Common name: Black broom.

Plant family:
Sterculiaceae (Cocoa family).

Growth Form:
Shrub to 3½ ft., somewhat weedy.

Range: Florida, Texas to Brazil, and throughout the West Indies.

Leaf: Alternate, ovate, about ½–1½ inches long, gray or silvery due to dense hairs on both sides, edges with rounded serrations.

Flower: Pink to lavender, 5-petalled, about ½ inch across.

Fruit: A 5-angled dry capsule, about one-quarter inch wide.

Stem/bark: Much branched, slender, dark brown and smooth.

Comments:

This pretty and very common shrub appears well adapted to colonizing disturbed areas, and since it is apparently unpalatable to goats it is thriving in present day East End. A weed, but a native weed, also found in relatively pristine sites.

Medicinal/economic uses: The plant is used in Cuba as a tea for colds, and in Jamaica as a cooling wash for eye infections.

Landscape use: Attractive flowering shrub for borders, low hedges, etc. Potentially a good soil stabilizer for steep arid areas.

Propagation: By seed or cuttings.

Growth rate: Moderate to fast.

Drought tolerance: Excellent.

Wind tolerance: Very good.

Salt tolerance: Fair

Conservation status: Not threatened.

Oplonia microphylla

Scientific name: *Oplonia microphylla*

Common name: Chuk bush.

Plant family: Acanthaceae (Acanthus family).

Growth form: Shrub with sprawling (sometimes vine-like) spiny branches.

Range: Jamaica to the Grenadines.

Leaf: Opposite or clustered at the nodes; very small, ¼–¾ inch by ⅒–¼ inch; somewhat shiny and stiff.

Flower: Blue, violet or lavender; funnel shaped, with 5 spreading lobes, one wider than the others; ¼–1 inch long.

Fruit: A narrow capsule about 1 inch long, containing 4 seeds.

Stem/bark: Stems to 6 ft. long, often forming tangled masses (generally much shorter on East End), with opposite straight or slightly curved sharp spines at each node.

Comments:

If this shrub produced its delicate bluish flowers more heavily or consistently, it would surely be a widely cultivated ornamental. As it is, the blooms are a fleeting pleasure. In spite of the impressive spines, goats consume the younger shoots; reducing many plants to stubby little mounds of tough stems. This is one of two plants often confused with the very rare Woodbury's machaonia on East End, differentiated when not in bloom by the opposite spines—not modified twigs as in Machaonia or twins joined at the base as in Scolosanthus.

Medicinal/economic use: None known.

Landscape use: Ornamental in bloom, useful as a soil stabilizer or as a barrier hedge for humans (although not for goats).

Propagation: By seeds or cuttings. **Growth rate:** Moderate to fast. **Drought tolerance:** Excellent.

Wind tolerance: Excellent. **Salt tolerance:** Good.

Conservation status: Not threatened.

Pictetia aculeata

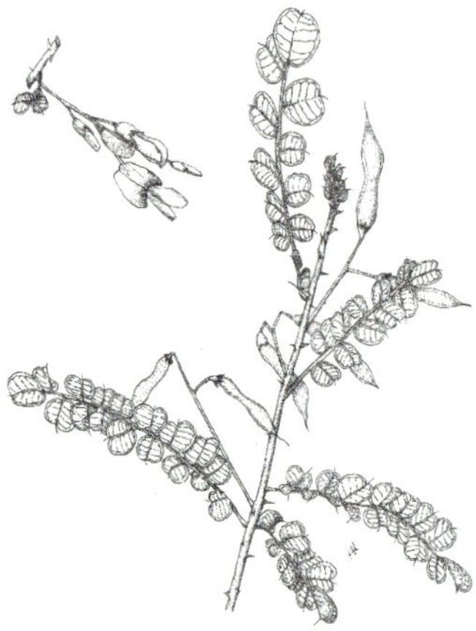

Scientific name: *Pictetia aculeata*

Common name: Fustic.

Plant family: Fabaceae, sub-family Faboideae (Pea sub-family).

Growth form: Shrub or small tree.

Range:
Puerto Rico and the Virgin Islands.

Leaf: Alternate; compound, with 9–25 leaflets; leaflets about ½ inch, rounded, shiny, curved up from the mid-rib, tipped by a yellowish spine.

Flower: Bright yellow, pea blossom-shaped, ¾–1 inch long, in clusters to 3 inches long.

Fruit:
Brown pod, flat, usually 1–2 inches long.

Stem/bark: Bark smooth, brown, peeling in flakes.

COMMENTS:

One of the prettiest flowering plants of arid regions of Puerto Rico and the V.I., fustic is worthy of admiration and cultivation. The very hard wood is similar to lignum vitae and was much used in the past, so most plants seen on St. John are relatively small. On the southwestern end of St. Thomas, in the Botany Bay area, individuals with 6–7 inch diameter trunks are common.

Medicinal/economic uses: A very closely related species, *Pictetia spinifolia*, is used in Cuba and Hispanola as a laxative and purgative and topically for sores, healing wounds and as a poultice for headaches. Fustic wood is not now of sufficient size to be used.

Landscape use: Very attractive shrub or small tree for gardens, street and roadside plantings or hedges.

Propagation: By seeds or cuttings of semi-hard wood. Cuttings best taken in spring or early summer.

Growth rate: Slow to moderate.

Drought tolerance: Exceptional

Wind tolerance: Very good.

Salt tolerance: Fair.

Conservation status: Not presently threatened, might become so in the future due to limited range and habitat.

Piptocoma antillana

Scientific name: *Piptocoma antillana*

Common name: None known.

Family name:
Asteraceae (Aster family).

Growth form:
Shrub, 1½–10 ft. tall, usually 3–5 ft.

Range:
Puerto Rico and Virgin Islands.

Leaf: Alternate on the stem, entire, 1–3 inches long x ¼–1 inch wide, gray-green and slightly hairy on the upper surface, often slightly rust-colored beneath.

Flower: At the branch ends, clusters of lavender blue brush-like composite heads; clusters to 3 inches across, flower heads about ¼ inch tall. Flowering intermittently throughout the year.

Fruit: Dry and tiny, with short light-brown hair-like attachments.

Trunk/bark: Twigs gray-green and somewhat fuzzy when young, becoming gray.

Comments:

Piptocoma is one of the commonest shrubs of the less disturbed sections of East End. It is unpalatable to goats and thus continues to thrive on the driest hills, where its silvery foliage and bluish flowers are conspicuous in the landscape. This species is endemic to Puerto Rico and the Northern Virgin Islands (not known on St. Croix).

Medicinal / economic uses: Not known. Many, if not most, members of this plant family are used medicinally in the Caribbean region.

Propagation methods: By seed or cuttings of medium-sized stems.

Landscape uses: Excellent shrub for gardens and low hedges, ever-blooming with irrigation.

Growth rate: Relatively fast.

Drought tolerance: Exceptional, once established.

Wind tolerance: Very good.

Salt tolerance: Fair.

Conservation status: Abundant in habitat. The very limited range may be increasingly restricted by development pressure.

Randia aculeata

Scientific name: *Randia aculeata*

Common names: Inkberry, Christmas tree, five-finger, fishing rod.

Plant family: Rubiaceae (Coffee family).

Growth form: Spiny semi-deciduous shrub or small tree.

Range: South Florida to Trinidad, Mexico to Venezuela.

Leaf: Opposite or clustered; variable in shape, often spoon-shaped; usually ½–1½ inches long and ¼–1 inch broad; shiny.

Flower: White, very fragrant, 5-lobed, slightly more than ½ inch across, single on very short side twigs along the branches.

Fruit: A rounded berry, ¼ to ½ inch across, white at maturity, containing several seeds in a dark blue or black inky pulp.

Stem/trunk: One to several upright trunks bearing many long horizontal branches with short side twigs that end in paired spines about ¼–½ inch long.

COMMENTS:

As the abundance of common names suggests, this is a very familiar shrub in the Virgin Islands. This, not the dry century plant flower, is the traditional Christmas tree of the islands, probably due to the often-conical shape, the nicely shiny leaves and the handy spines for attaching ornaments. The flowers have a powerful fragrance reminiscent of the related gardenia.

Medicinal/economic uses: A dark blue dye has been made from the berries, which are also reported to be edible. The fruit have been used to treat dysentery, the leaves made a tea for fever, and the sap is reportedly effective in clotting blood.

Landscape use: Great fragrant flowering shrub. May be pruned into dense hedges; the spines are fairly formidable, even to goats.

Propagation: By seed, or, less reliably, by cuttings or air layers. **Growth rate:** Slow to moderate.

Drought tolerance: Excellent. **Wind tolerance:** Excellent. **Salt tolerance:** Good.

Conservation status: Not threatened.

Rondeletia pilosa

Scientific name: *Rondeletia pilosa*

Common name: Downy rondeletia, wild rondeletia.

Plant family: Rubiaceae (Coffee family).

Growth form: Woody shrub.

Range: Puerto Rico and the Virgin Islands.

Leaf: Opposite, 1 to 3 inches long and ½ to 1½ inches wide, with short flattened hairs on upper surface and soft hairs beneath; side veins conspicuous, long curved, sunken.

Flower: Dusty pink to mauve or grayish, tiny, with a long tube and 4 lobes, usually in clusters of 3 on ¾ to 2 inch long stalks, extremely fragrant at night, scentless in daylight.

Fruit: A round capsule, less than ¼ inch across, containing many tiny seeds.

Stem/bark: Many-stemmed from base; bark smooth, gray; twigs hairy, cylindrical.

Comments: The genus Rondeletia has about 120 species in tropical America, some of which are colorful and widely cultivated ornamentals. Our Puerto Rico and Virgin Island native is unassuming, and one might overlook the oddly colored little flowers altogether, but...the nocturnal fragrance of these tiny blooms is one of the most glorious in the world—full and rich, yet not overly sweet or cloying.

Medicinal/economic uses: None known.

Landscape use: The foliage is attractive enough to merit placement in full view and the fragrance is a great bonus. Although adapted to very dry areas, wild rondeletia prefers a north exposure or protection from full sun.

Propagation: By the minute seeds, barely covered with fine potting medium; or by cuttings or airlayers.

Growth rate: Moderate. **Drought tolerance:** Very good.

Wind tolerance: Fair. **Salt tolerance:** Fair.

Conservation status: Not threatened, but its very limited range (it is reportedly quite rare in Puerto Rico) adds to the value of conserving this worthy species.

Schaefferia frutescens

Scientific name: *Schaefferia frutescens*

Common name: Yellow boxwood.

Plant family:
Celastraceae. (Bittersweet family).

Growth form:
Woody evergreen shrub.

Range: Florida to Grenada and Mexico to Venezuela.

Leaf: Alternate, usually yellow-green, elliptic, 1–2 inches long and ½–1 inch broad, somewhat stiff and leathery, often turned up strongly on either side of the mid-vein, tip usually very sharply pointed.

Flower: Male and female on separate plants, both tiny, yellow-green, 4-parted.

Fruit: Orange-red, round or oval, less than ¼ inch in diameter, containing 1–2 woody light brown seeds.

Stem/bark: Bark light gray, variable from smooth to fissured or furrowed; twigs slender, green.

Comments:

This common shrub thrives in many different habitats in the Virgin Islands, but is most noticeable in dry areas, where the foliage may become very yellow-green but remains intact through the dry months. Like several other local members of the bittersweet family, this is not eaten by goats, although lacking any spines or known toxins.

Medicinal/economic uses: The plant is believed to be an aphrodisiac in Cuba and Haiti, and is also used as a remedy for gripe, cataracts, chronic coughs and as a bath for skin irritations. Additionally the leaves have been used as soap for the body and to launder clothes. The hard and heavy yellowish wood has been used as a substitute for boxwood where the stems grow larger than they do locally.

Landscape use: Good dense shrub for screening, hedges or soil stabilization. Looks best when grown in partial shade.

Propagation: By seeds.

Growth rate: Moderate.

Drought tolerance: Excellent.

Wind tolerance: Very good.

Salt tolerance: Very good.

Conservation status: Not threatened.

Scolosanthus versicolor

Scientific name: *Scolosanthus versicolor*

Common name: None known.

Plant family: Rubiaceae (Coffee family).

Growth form: Erect evergreen shrub, 2–8 ft.

Range: Puerto Rico and the Virgin Islands.

Leaf: Opposite, but appearing to be whorled due to close spacing; tiny, about ¼ inch long; ovate or spoon-shaped; stiff, very dark green and shiny.

Flower: Less than ½ inch long; tubular, with 4 lobes; yellow streaked with maroon or black.

Fruit: White, oval to globose; about ¼ inch long; containing one seed.

Stem/bark: Twigs slender and cylindrical, green when young, with paired reddish-brown spines.

Comments:

This prickly shrub is one of some charm on close examination. Both the oddly colored tiny flowers and the bright white berries are unusual and contrast well with the minute glossy foliage. The plant is not especially common on East End, but is included here due to frequent confusion with the rare *Machaonia woodburyana.* The main distinguishing point, if the plants are not in bloom, is the arrangement of the spines: forked, Y- or V-shaped in *Scolosanthus,* opposite or at the tip of short side branches in *Machaonia.*

Medicinal/economic uses: None known.

Landscape use: Slow growth and dense spiny branching make this ideal for barrier hedges, etc. Needs shade or north exposure to look its best.

Propagation: By seed or air layering.

Growth rate: Slow.

Drought tolerance: Excellent, with some shade.

Wind tolerance: Very good.

Salt tolerance: Poor.

Conservation status: Not threatened; should be conserved where possible due to limited geographic range.

Turnera diffusa

Scientific name: *Turnera diffusa*

Common names:
Old woman's broom, damiana.

Family name:
Turneraceae (Turnera family).

Growth form: Shrub to 2 ft., often much lower due to goat browsing.

Range: Continental tropical America, West Indies from the Bahamas to Virgin Islands.

Leaf: Alternate on the stems, often in tight clusters on short side branches; very small, ¼ to ½ inch long, 0.10 to ¼ inch broad; densely covered with short silvery hairs; margins serrate, wavy; distinctly aromatic when crushed. Very similar to the foliage of several other plants in this habitat, distinguished by the small size and strong herbal odor.

Flower: Almost stemless at the tips of the short branches, bright yellow, less than ½ inch across, with five petals and inconspicuous stamens. Flowering all year except in drought.

Fruit: A three-valved capsule, about ¼ inch long; splitting open at maturity, with numerous brown dust-like seeds.

COMMENTS:

This sub-shrub is characteristic of the less disturbed arid and rocky areas of the region. The silvery appearance, mounding habit and strong herbal aroma combine in a most attractive fashion. Goats browse on the younger shoots but usually do not kill the plants totally.

Propagation methods: By the tiny seeds (barely cover with light potting soil, keep bright and barely moist); or by 3-inch cuttings of older stems, in light potting soil or pure perlite.

Medicinal/economic uses: In the Virgin Islands a fragrant tea has been used to combat menopausal symptoms (hence the "old woman's broom"); here and elsewhere the tea is also highly regarded as a male aphrodisiac and impotence cure. Teas have also been used to treat nervous complaints, afflictions of the kidneys and bladder, and indigestion. Also used in refreshing baths.

Landscape uses: Ideal rock garden plant, ground cover for very exposed situations.

Growth rate: Slow. **Drought tolerance:** Exceptional.

Wind tolerance: Very good. **Salt tolerance:** Medium.

Conservation needs: This species appears to be confined to arid slopes that historically were little exploited. It does not re-colonize disturbed areas readily, perhaps due to slow growth and inability to compete with weedy species. On St. John both the plant and its habitat are under pressure from feral goats (East End, Ram Head) and subdivision development (East End, Chocolate Hole). Preservation of habitat is key.

VINES

Capparis flexuosa

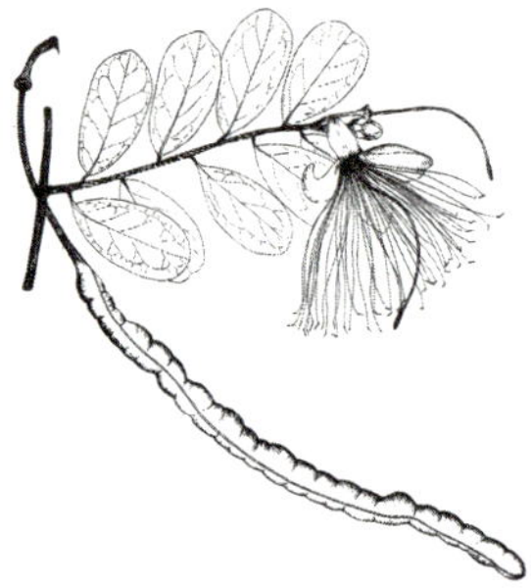

Scientific name: *Capparis flexuosa* **Common name:** Limber caper.

Plant family: Capparaceae (Caper family).

Growth form: Very woody vine, almost a shrub. **Range:** Florida to Argentina.

Leaf: Alternate, leathery; shape extremely variable, oval, oblong or linear; usually 2–4 inches long and ½ to 1 inch wide; sometimes longer and much narrower, especially on seedlings.

Flower: Nocturnal, opening around dusk and disintegrating the following morning; large, white, with 4 short petals and numerous 2–3 inch long filament-like stamens, fragrant.

Fruit: A pendant pod, cylindrical, 3–8 inches long and ½ inch across, greenish with red lines when near maturity, opening to reveal a dark red lining and white seeds.

Stem/bark: Stems woody but usually long and vine like, climbing over other vegetation for support.

COMMENTS:

A common component of the dry forest vegetation, limber caper is unassuming in the daylight but a real show at night. Moths pollinate the fragrant brush-like blooms and bats consume the thin white flesh around the seeds.

Medicinal/economic use: The fruit has been used as an anti-spasmodic, the bark as a diuretic, the leaves in baths for skin problems and the root as treatment for dropsy. The root is reported to have a flavor similar to horseradish.

Landscape use: A tough and sturdy plant with ornamental value. Given space to sprawl can be very useful as a cover or informal hedge.

Propagation: By fresh seeds, collected just as pods are splitting open. **Growth rate:** Moderate to fast.

Drought tolerance: Exceptional. **Wind tolerance:** Very good.

Salt tolerance: Very good. **Conservation status:** Not threatened.

Ipomoea eggersii

Scientific name: *Ipomoea eggersii*

Common name: Jumbie potato.

Family name: Convolvulaceae (Morning glory family).

Growth form:
Slender twining vine to 15 ft.

Range:
Virgin Islands and Lesser Antilles.

Leaf: Very small, crowded on short side branches; ¼–¾ inch by 0.10–½ inch; wildly variable in shape, oval, or fiddle-shaped, usually more or less deeply 2 or more-lobed; the tip notched, with a tiny pointed projection in the center.

Flower: Funnel-shaped; 1½ to 2 inches long, 1 to 2 inches wide; pink or light purple, ephemeral. Flowering year round except during prolonged drought.

Fruit: A light brown capsule, ½ inch long, containing 4 dark brown seeds about ¼ inch long.

Trunk/bark: Stems slender, cylindrical, green or reddish, containing copious milky sap. Roots produce numerous large (to 8 x 5 inch) tubers, resembling the related sweet potato (*Ipomoea batatas*).

COMMENTS:

The lovely and relatively large pale pink flowers of this morning glory appear in the driest areas of the V.I., often in near drought conditions when no other plants have the energy to produce blooms. The secret of success is the hidden underground tubers, storage for nutrients and moisture through the long and frequent droughts. The distinctively shaped leaves are tiny in relation to the flowers, an unusual occurrence in the entire plant kingdom.

Medicinal/economic uses: Not known.

Propagation methods: By seeds.

Landscape uses: Small ornamental vine, suitable for training on posts, etc.

Growth rate: Fast, with water. **Drought tolerance**: Exceptional. **Wind tolerance**: Good.

Salt tolerance: Moderate. **Conservation needs**: Not threatened.

Jacquemontia pentanthos

Scientific name: *Jacquemontia pentanthos*

Common names: Clashie-malashie, wild morning glory.

Plant family: Convolvulaceae (Morning glory family).

Growth form: Slender twining vine.

Range: Most of tropical America.

Leaf: Alternate; 1 to 2 inches long and ¾ to 1½ inches wide; often heart-shaped; with short sparse white hairs.

Flower: Bright blue with star-shaped white center, about 1 inch across, in clusters from the leaf axils.

Fruit: A dry capsule, less than ¼ inch long, containing 4 small seeds.

Stem/bark: Stem slender, twining, to about 7 ft. long.

COMMENTS:

This diminutive morning glory can be breathtaking when covered with masses of deep blue blooms.

Medicinal/economic uses: None known.

Landscape uses: Beautiful small vine for low fences, walls, etc.

Propagation: By seed or by cuttings of woodier stems.

Growth rate: Fast. **Drought tolerance:** Very good. **Wind tolerance:** Very good.

Salt tolerance: Fair. **Conservation status:** Not threatened.

Pentalinon luteum

Scientific name: *Pentalinon luteum*

Common name: Wild allamanda.

Plant family: Apocynaceae (Dogbane family).

Growth form: Slender woody vine.

Range: South Florida to the Grenadines.

Leaf: Opposite, elliptic; 1 to 3 inches long, ½ to 1½ inches wide; somewhat shiny.

Flower: Bright yellow, about 2 inches long and broad; bell-shaped, with 5 rounded lobes; reddish brown stripes within the throat.

Fruit: Twin pods, joined at the tip, 5–7 inches long, dark brown when ripe, containing many wind-distributed seeds with attached "parachutes".

Stem/bark: Stem branched near the base, twining; to 18 feet long, usually shorter; bark smooth reddish-brown with many raised white spots (lenticles).

COMMENTS:

A cultivated form of this slender vine has been introduced from Florida and is now often seen in V.I. gardens, bearing more abundant and slightly larger blooms than our native form, but apparently not quite as tough. Like many members of its family, this is a toxic plant if consumed, and should be handled carefully and kept away from very young children.

Medicinal/economic uses: In spite of the strong toxins present, this has been used internally as a remedy for dropsy and syphilis, and externally in baths for persistent sores.

Landscape uses: This is an excellent choice for trellises and screening, especially in exposed coastal conditions. Tolerates sandy soil very well.

Propagation: By either cuttings or seeds.

Growth rate: Fast. **Drought tolerance:** Very good. **Salt tolerance:** Excellent.

Wind tolerance: Excellent **Conservation status:** Not threatened.

Stigmaphyllon emarginatum

Scientific name:
Stigmaphyllon emarginatum

Common names:
Yellow wiss, leatherleaf.

Plant family: Malpighiaceae (Barbados cherry family).

Growth form: Woody vine (liana).

Range: Hispanola to St. Lucia.

Leaf: Opposite, usually elliptic, 2 to 3 inches long and 1 to 2 inches broad, thick and leathery, often with conspicuous net-patterned veins.

Flower: Yellow, somewhat over 1 inch across, with 5 delicate petals, in large clusters. Appearing abundantly with spring rains, but also sporadically at other times.

Fruit: Flat winged samaras, similar to maple seeds, reddish when young, about 1 inch long.

Stem/bark: Rope-like vine often twined around itself, bark coppery brown and stringy. Can grow to 50 feet and over 2 inches in stem diameter.

Comments:

Rivaling any exotic garden flowering vine in its beauty, this is also one of the toughest native plants around, thriving in just about every location in the Virgin Islands, including cliffs and offshore cays with little other vegetation.

Flowering is best with spring rains following a late winter drought, but some blooms may appear at almost any time of year. The first several sets of leaves on seedlings may be remarkably different, with silvery veins against a deep olive or blackish background. Many people have attempted to transplant one of these little gems, only to have the leaves mature quickly to plain green.

Medicinal/economic uses: Reported to be used as a dandruff treatment and as a tonic tea.

Landscape use: Excellent vine for covering unsightly areas and for use in ornamental plantings.

Propagation: By the winged seeds, collected when they are just dry and beginning to blow away.

Growth rate: Fast. **Drought tolerance:** Exceptional. **Wind tolerance:** Exceptional.

Salt tolerance: Exceptional. **Conservation status:** Not threatened.

Cactus, Succulents and Epiphytes

Agave missionum

Scientific name: *Agave missionum*

Common names:
Century plant, karata.

Family name: Agavaceae (Century plant family).

Growth form:
Large succulent shrub.

Range: Puerto Rico and the Virgin Islands excluding St. Croix.

Leaf: Very succulent, sword-shaped, stemless, 2½ to 8 feet. long on mature plants, edged with dark brown triangular spines.

Flower: A gigantic panicle, 15 to 24 feet tall, with many lateral branches in the upper half to two-thirds bearing abundant bright yellow 2½ inch blooms in dense clusters. Spring to early summer.

Fruit: Dry capsules; containing numerous black, flat, triangular seeds, about ½ inch long.

Bark/stem: Plant theoretically stemless, but aged individuals may have several feet of exposed stem at the base where older leaves have fallen.

COMMENTS:

One of the cornerstone species of the dryland vegetation of the Virgin Islands. The flowers have great importance in the sustenance of innumerable native birds, insects and bats. Generally appearing during the driest days of the year in early spring, these enormous panicles provide a veritable cornucopia of nectar at a time when little else is available.

Although this has been one of the commonest and seemingly unthreatened of native plants, the larva of a weevil (apparently introduced with ornamental plant shipments from south Florida) has recently been devastating Virgin Islands plants. First seen on St. Thomas in 1994, this pest has spread to Tortola by 2000 and St. John by 2001, being particularly lethal in the Haulover Bay area as of 2002.

The use of the dried flower stalks as Christmas trees is a recent tradition, probably originating with early continental settlers in the mid-20th century.

Medicinal/economic uses: The sap of the leaves is very irritating to the skin and mucus membranes, but a decoction of the roots has reportedly been used as a laxative and diuretic. The fibers of the leaves are very strong, similar to those of sisal (*Agave sisaliana*); there have been proposals for commercial production in the past that never got off the ground.

Propagation methods: By seeds or adventitious plantlets that may be produced on the flower stems a month or two after flowering.

Landscape uses: Specimen, hedge, barrier, soil retainer on steep slopes.

Growth rate: Moderate to fast.

Drought tolerance: Exceptional.

Wind tolerance: Exceptional.

Salt tolerance: Very good.

Conservation status: Extremely threatened in the very near future by the agave weevil (see above). This pest is known for attacking mature plants of various agave species in its native Mexico and elsewhere, in these cases the plants are already reproducing and little harm is done to the overall population. Our endemic agave is being killed at all ages, and no practical control is evident. Adult weevils can apparently fly the short distances between islands and cays in the Northern Virgin Islands.

Melocactus intortus

Scientific name: *Melocactus intortus*

Common names: Turk's cap, Pope's head, barrel cactus.

Plant family: Cactaceae (Cactus family).

Growth form: Succulent, barrel-shaped, technically a shrub.

Range: West Indies.

Leaf: Leafless.

Flower: Bright pink, tubular, about I inch long, several arranged in a spiral on the top of the wooly " head" of the cactus.

Fruit: Bright pink, up to I inch long, club-shaped, the juicy white flesh filled with numerous tiny black seeds. Edible and refreshing on a hot day, pleasant although not exactly flavorful.

Bark/stem: Cylindrical or ball shaped, to about 2½ ft. tall, mature specimens topped by one or more cylindrical head (cephalum) covered with white fibers. Spines on main plant stout, pale; on cephalum small, reddish.

COMMENTS:

This distinctive cactus is commonest on the dry coastal rocks of the region, but may also be found inland in extremely arid areas. The plants acquire unique shapes with age and are often endearingly full of character, seeming almost animal-like in their poses on the rocky landscape.

The colorful fruit and flowers are designed to be highly visible to birds—the hummingbirds that hover to pollinate and many other species that consume the fruit and spread the seeds. Lizards, iguanas and rodents also consume the fruits. Feral goats sometimes manage to break into the juicy interior of the plant, this is usually fatal.

Medicinal/economic uses: None known.

Propagation methods: By seed, which is easily collected by drying the juicy fruit. Seeds should be just barely covered with very fine well-drained soil. Seed flats and young seedlings need to be kept slightly moist and protected from rain. It is reported that the plants prefer alkaline soils and the addition of ground limestone to the planting mix or soil is recommended. Mature plants do not transplant easily from the wild; thousands have probably met untimely deaths from ignorant attempts to move them into gardens.

Landscape uses: Ornamental, particularly suited to rock gardens and extremely exposed sites. Requires full sun. The root system is surprisingly extensive and plantings may be effective as soil stabilizers on steep dry slopes.

Growth rate: Slow.

Drought tolerance: Exceptional.

Wind tolerance: Exceptional.

Salt tolerance: Excellent.

Conservation status: Still fairly abundant in the VI. Threats include horticultural collection and habitat disturbance by construction—and ever-increasing feral goat populations.

Opuntia dillenii

Scientific name: *Opuntia dillenii*

Common names:
Prickly pear, Miss Blyden.

Plant family:
Cactaceae (Cactus family).

Growth form: Shrub.

Range: Southeast U.S., Mexico and throughout the West Indies.

Leaf: Leafless.

Flower: Yellow, 2 to 3 inches long and wide.

Fruit: Red, pear-shaped or oval, 2 to 2½ inches long, with clusters of tiny spines, edible.

Bark/stem: Pads rounded; with sturdy yellowish spines 1–2¾ inches long, in groups of 3–7.

COMMENTS:

This well-known prickly pear is much less frequently seen on St. John than formerly, perhaps due to predation by the caterpillar of the introduced *Cactoblastis* moth. These small orange caterpillars were used as an effective biological control of invasive Opuntia species in Australia and Asia, unfortunately the caterpillar is now killing native opuntias in the Caribbean.

Medicinal/economic uses: Both the fruits and the pads are edible. The small spines of the fruits can be avoided by slicing open and peeling back the skin. The pads are more palatable when roasted; they have also been used as a dressing for wounds, for washing the hair and in treatment of headaches, earaches and inflammation.

Landscape use: Handsome cactus for rock gardens, borders, hedges; recommended for stabilization of cut-banks etc.

Propagation: By cuttings of the pads, taken at the joint; or (with patience) by seed.

Growth rate: Slow to moderate. **Drought tolerance:** Exceptional.

Wind tolerance: Excellent. **Salt tolerance:** Excellent.

Conservation status: Much less common than in the past, should be conserved wherever possible.

Opuntia rubescens

Scientific name: *Opuntia rubescens*

Common names:
Tree prickly pear, blyden bush.

Plant family:
Cactaceae (Cactus family).

Growth form: Shrub or small tree.

Range: Puerto Rico to Guadeloupe.

Leaf: Leafless.

Flower: Yellow-orange to orange, about ¾ inch across, appearing at the end of a green spiny ovary about 2 inches long.

Fruit: Red, pear-shaped or oval, about 2½ inches long, usually very spiny.

Stem/bark: Forming a cylindrical trunk with gray or reddish flaking bark and long gray spines.

COMMENTS:

This tree prickly pear is easily distinguishable by its elongated pads, numerous spines and tree-like form.

Medicinal/economic uses: None known, presumably similar to *Opuntia dillenii.*

Landscape uses: Interesting specimen plant, could be used for a formidable tall hedge. Good soil stabilizer for extremely dry areas.

Propagation: By cuttings of the pads (very easy) or by seed (slow and difficult).

Growth rate: Slow.

Drought tolerance: Superb.

Wind tolerance: Exceptional.

Salt tolerance: Very good.

Conservation status:
Not threatened.

Pilosocereus royenii

Scientific name: *Pilosocereus royenii*

Common names: Diddledoo, dildo, pipe-organ cactus.

Plant family: Cactaceae (Cactus family).

Growth form: Shrub or small tree.

Range: Puerto Rico to Antigua.

Leaf: Leafless.

Flower: More-or-less white, tubular, 2–3 inches long, stalkless, opening at night.

Fruit: Red, rounded, about 1½–2 inches across, smooth, edible, containing many tiny black seeds.

Stem/bark Lower trunk brown; branches gray-green to blue green, columnar; approximately 3 inches in diameter; with 7–11 ribs bearing groups of sharp yellow or gray spines, these generally ¾ to 2 inches long.

COMMENTS:

The most conspicuous cactus in the Virgin Islands landscape, these attractive tall bluish columns appear wherever conditions are dry enough, including rocky coasts and outcrops on the moist north shores.

Medicinal/economic use: Not known. The fruit are juicy and sweet but difficult to harvest.

Landscape use: Dramatic large cactus, excellent in rock gardens and steep cliff-sides. Useful as a stabilizer on banks and cliffs.

Propagation: By cuttings of smaller branches (allow to callus at the cut end for a week or two) or by seeds.

Growth rate: Generally slow, can make surprising leaps during wet periods or following storm damage.

Drought tolerance: Unparalleled.

Wind tolerance: Exceptional.

Salt tolerance: Excellent.

Conservation status: Not threatened.

Psychilis macconnelliae

Scientific name: *Psychilis macconnelliae*

Common names: Butterfly orchid, bullfoot orchid.

Family name:
Orchidaceae (Orchid family).

Growth form: Epiphytic herb, growing in clumps on rocks and small trees.

Range: Puerto Rico to St. Kitts.

Leaf: Two–4 per pseudobulb, leathery, stiff, usually 5–8 inches long and ¾–1¼ inch wide.

Flower: About 2 inches across; mostly lavender or pink with white markings on the broad lip, with some olive green on the two petals and three sepals, which are similar to one another. Flowering in small clusters at the end of very thin spikes (scapes) 1½–5 ft. long. Blooms all year.

Fruit: A green to yellow-brown capsule, elliptic, 1–1¾ inches long; splitting open at maturity to reveal a powdery mass of minute whitish or light brown seeds.

Trunk/stem: Sub-cylindrical pseudobulbs 5–8 inches long, yellowish-green, arising in clumps from short rhizomes and exposed white or gray roots.

COMMENTS:

One of the two most common of St. John's twelve native orchid species, this is the only orchid seen frequently on the East End, especially in the more pristine areas such as Privateer Bay. The extremely long flower spikes often serve to hold the blooms up above the surrounding low vegetation, where they are more visible to their flying pollinators. These flower spikes may continue to produce new blossoms for several years, branching from successively lower nodes. Although it thrives under apparently harsh conditions, like almost all epiphytic orchids this species is very sensitive to alteration of its narrow environmental niche. Goats are destroying many plants on the East End.

Medicinal/economic uses: Not known.

Propagation methods: Although there are over 100,000 seeds in each pod, these minute specks are very difficult to germinate. In nature, each species of epiphytic orchid has a special relationship with a member of a group of fungi, which provides the nutrition needed for early growth. Modern orchid growers use nutrient media under sterile conditions, a costly and rather difficult undertaking.

All indigenous orchids are protected under Virgin Island law, and should never be removed from the wild. Many people do cultivate this species in gardens, and small clumps of at least three pseudobulbs may be separated and established on trees and rocks.

Landscape uses: Very attractive small epiphyte, everblooming. Blooms best with at least a half day of full sunlight.

Growth rate: Slow. Does respond to moderate watering and fertilizing provided drainage is excellent.

Drought tolerance: Excellent, once established.

Wind tolerance: Good.

Salt tolerance: Moderate.

Conservation needs: While this orchid is still relatively common on St. John and some of the BVI, many plants are lost annually to construction activity, human poaching and feral animal grazing. On East End, efforts to remove wild goats and education of property owners may help preserve this beautiful plant for the future.

Tillandsia utriculata

Scientific name: *Tillandsia utriculata*

Common names: Air plant, wild pine, common tillandsia.

Plant family: Bromeliaceae (Pineapple family).

Growth form: Rosette-formed epiphytic herb.

Range: Florida; Mexico to Venezuela and throughout the West Indies.

Leaf: Long and tapering, 15–30 inches long on mature plants; grayish, stiff, arranged in a rosette.

Flower: An erect branched spike from the center of the plant, 2–5 ft. high, bearing green or yellowish (occasionally purplish) bracts that contain the quarter-inch-long pale yellow flowers.

Fruit: Dry capsules on the old spikes, containing numerous tiny seeds with attached silky-haired "parachutes" 1 –1½ inches long.

Stem/bark: Short, hidden by the leaf bases, not branching or off-setting.

COMMENTS:

There are between 400–500 different species of *Tillandsia* in Tropical America, many with colorful flowers and striking silvery foliage.

This, the most common in the Virgin Islands, is a relatively drab species, but extremely important in native ecosystems. Like many of the members of the bromeliad family, this is an epiphyte, growing happily on trees, rocks, or the bare ground of the driest areas. The plant captures rainfall in the pockets between the leaf bases, absorbing moisture in this fashion more than through the roots. Water remains in these small wells long after a rain, providing drinks to birds and other animals, and breeding spots for many insect species and our (tadpole-less) native tree frogs. The plant only blooms once at maturity, goes to seed and dies, like the much larger and unrelated century plant.

Medicinal/economic uses: None known.

Landscape uses: Highly decorative on trees and rock formations. Attracts many hummingbirds when in bloom. Plants may be attached to trees with wire, or simply wedged between rocks. The roots should not be buried in the ground.

Propagation: By the seeds, which are available in quantity on the recently flowered plants. Germination is best on moist but very well drained surfaces, such as pieces of treefern fiber or tree bark.

Growth rate: Slow.

Drought tolerance: Excellent, especially if given light shade.

Wind tolerance: Fair to good.

Salt tolerance: Fair.

Conservation status: Not threatened.

Common Non-Natives

These six species are abundant and conspicuous in the East End landscape.

In most cases they have been here for many years. The toxic species are certainly becoming more common as goats allow them to proliferate while consuming any competition.

Photo: *Tamarindus indica* in bloom.

Antigonon leptopus

Scientific name: *Antigonon leptopus*

Common name: Coral vine, coralita, Mexican creeper, "honeysuckle".

Plant family: Polygonaceae (Buckwheat family).

Native to:
Mexico and Central America.

A pretty but very aggressive vine, this was originally brought in as a garden plant. The extensive tuberous root systems are very difficult to remove and the vine will happily resprout no matter how frequently it is taken back to the ground, either by cutting or dying back in extended droughts. It apparently persists anywhere it has ever been planted in the Virgin Islands.

Calotropis procera

Scientific name: *Calotropis procera*

Common name: Giant milkweed, cow-heel.

Plant family: Asclepiadaceae (Milkweed family).

Native to: Africa.

A poisonous ornamental plant that becomes commoner in grazed areas, giant milkweed is now a weed in many parts of the world tropics. Goats have been observed eating this in small quantities.

Cryptostegia grandiflora

Scientific name: *Cryptostegia grandiflora.*

Common name: Rubber vine, purple allamanda (a misnomer, since it is not related).

Plant family: Asclepiadaceae (Milkweed family).

Native to: Africa.

Introduced as a hardy garden plant, probably in the early 20th century, this attractive woody vine is toxic to livestock and extremely tolerant of drought and saline soils—a combination that is aiding its spread in Coral Bay and on the East End. The thick milky sap (latex) was used as a rubber substitute during World War II, when the Japanese had taken over the global supply of rubber, the product of a South American tree then grown commercially only in Malaysia. If rubber vine is grown as an ornamental, care should be taken to trim it back very regularly, to remove the slow-maturing seedpods before they can distribute their numerous wind-borne seeds.

Euphorbia tirucalli

Scientific name: *Euphorbia tirucalli*

Common name: Pencil bush, pencil "cactus", milk bush.

Plant family: Euphorbiaceae (Poinsettia family).

Native to: Africa.

This African succulent is often planted as a drought-tolerant screen, a job it does only too well—spreading and persisting forever unless someone has the fortitude to deal with the extremely caustic sap and remove the plant. And burn it, since cut branches will root and grow wherever they sit, except, perhaps, on concrete.

Not everyone has a reaction to the sap, but those that do are generally very profoundly affected.

Jatropha gossypifolia

Scientific name: *Jatropha gossypifolia*

Common name: Wild physicnut, belly ache bush.

Plant family: Euphorbiaceae (Poinsettia family).

Native to: Central America.

A very common low shrubby weed, particularly frequent on roadsides and other heavily disturbed areas. Wild physicnut is extensively used as a purgative and cleanser of the intestinal tract (use extreme caution).

Tamarindus indica

Scientific name: *Tamarindus indica*

Common name: Indian tamarind.
Plant family: Fabaceae, subfamily Caesalpinioideae (Cassia subfamily of Legume family).
Native to: India, now widespread throughout the tropics.

Obviously long established in the Virgin Islands, tamarinds were planted for shade and the very flavorful (and mouth puckering) sour fruits. The beautiful East End tamarinds are among the largest in the territory, some of them certainly over 200 years old. Many East End trees had branches repeatedly chopped for charcoal production. Tamarinds have been revered as "spirit trees" in many parts of the world. The trees have shown little sign of spreading into undisturbed areas of East End. It is reported that donkeys consume the seedlings.

Glossary

ALTERNATE – Referring to leaves or stems, arranged at different levels on either side of a main stem; not opposite.

AXIL – Usually referring to the point of attachment between a leaf or flower stem and the main stem of a plant; the upper angle formed by these.

BIPINNATE – Twice-pinnate, with leaflets arranged feather-fashion and several of these structures attached to a main central leaf stem.

BRACT – Modified leaf associated with the flower, sometimes colorful and petal-like, as in bougainvillea.

CAPSULE – A dry fruit that splits open at maturity, containing two or more seed housings.

CALYX – The outer part of the flower envelope, often covering the flower in the bud, composed of sepals that may be green or colored.

CEPHALUM – A wooly protrusion that supports the flowers and fruit at the top of some cacti.

COMPOUND – Made up of two or more usually similar parts, as in compound leaves composed of two or more leaflets.

CONICAL – Cone-shaped.

DECIDUOUS – Dropping foliage. In temperate climates associated with winter dormancy, in the tropics either associated with drought dormancy or the late winter preparation for the new growth that will commence with longer spring days.

DENTATE – Referring to leaf margins with sharp teeth that are at right angles to the central vein of the leaf.

DIOECIOUS – With male and female flowers on separate plants. Compare monoecious.

ENDEMIC – Native only to a certain restricted area.

ENTIRE – Not divided in any way, as in leaves margins without teeth or other protrusions.

ELLIPTIC – In the shape of an ellipse; oblong with rounded ends, widest around the middle.

EPIPHYTE – A plant that grows on another plant but is not parasitic, deriving no nutrition from the host. Most epiphytes also may grow on rocks, or even on the surface of the ground in extremely arid places.

EVERGREEN – Not deciduous, with foliage that remains green through more than one growing season. In the tropics generally those plants that retain all or most of their leaves through seasonal droughts. Some local evergreen trees will drop all leaves during extremely prolonged drought.

FAMILY – A group of genera (see genus) that share enough characteristics to be placed together. Some plant families contain a single genus or even a single species, while others are extremely large and may be broken down into sub-families based on various attributes. Recent genetic research may soon rearrange many long-accepted family groupings. See genus and species.

GENUS (plural genera) – A group of closely related plant species with common characteristics within a family. A genus may contain one to hundreds of species. The genus name is the first part of the two-part scientific name. Thus, the figs are the large genus *Ficus,* in the Moraceae or mulberry family, which includes the edible fig, *Ficus carica,* the weeping fig, *Ficus benjamina,* and so on. Many genus names have become the common name for groups of plants, as in hibiscus, bougainvillea, petunia, iris, begonia, etc. See family and species.

GLAND – A structure on stems, leaves, etc. that secretes oils, nectar or other substances; a gland-like body.

GLOBOSE – Rounded, spherical.

HEAD – A compound flower structure composed of stemless flowers densely grouped.

HERB – A plant without woody stems, often annual or dying back to the roots seasonally.

HERBACEOUS – With the attributes of a herb.

INDIGENOUS – Native; naturally occurring in a certain area, not introduced by humans either intentionally or accidentally.

INFLORESCENCE – The flowering structure of the plant, including the stems and any appendages.

LANCEOLATE – Spear-shaped; long, narrow and tapering at the ends, the base generally the widest part.

LATERAL – To the side.

LATEX – A water soluble liquid, usually milky but sometimes clear or colored, produced by the cells of some plants. "Milky sap".

LENTICLE – Warty areas, generally small, on the surface of stems or other plant parts.

LIANA – A woody tropical vine, usually long and high-climbing.

LICHEN – Described as one of the greatest puzzles in biology, lichens are symbiotic assemblages of at least two organisms, at least one of which is a fungus; the others may be algae or bacteria. Lichens occur in many different forms and almost every habitat on earth. Their sensitivity to stresses such as pollution makes them increasingly useful in monitoring the health of ecosystems.

LINEAR – Line-like; long narrow and straight, like blades of grass.

LIP – In orchids, a modified petal that is usually larger and far more ornate and colorful than the other flower parts. This serves as a target for pollinating insects guiding them directly to the nectar and pollen.

MARGIN – The edge of a leaf or petal.

MONECIOUS – With separate male and female flowers on the same plant. See dioecious.

NATIVE – Naturally occurring, not introduced.

NATURALIZED – Referring to non-native plants that are self-perpetuating, and generally expanding their range without human assistance.

NODE – The point on a stem where a leaf is attached or has been attached.

OBOVATE – Of an oval that is broader above the middle, inversely ovate

OVATE – Egg-shaped, oval, rounded at the ends and widest below the middle.

PALMATE – With more than two lobes, veins or segments radiating from a common point.

PANICLE – An inflorescence with a branched main stem and stemmed flowers borne on the secondary branches.

PINNA (plural pinnae) – A primary leaflet or division of a pinnately compound leaf. If the leaf is bi-pinnate, the secondary leaflets are called pinnules.

PINNATE – Feather shaped.

POD – A dry fruit, usually long and thin with several seeds as in most of the Fabaceae family; not a very specific word.

PSEUDOBULB – A thickened stem, varying from globose to cylindrical in shape, found in many orchids.

RECURVED – Curved down or back.

RHIZOME – An underground or reclining root-like stem.

ROSETTE – A cluster of leaves radiating from a common center, generally on a very short stem.

SAMARA – A dry fruit, usually one-seeded, with one or more wings, transported by wind.

SCAPE – A leafless flower stalk arising from the ground or from a short stem with leaves at the base.

SCRUB – Low vegetation limited in growth by drought, wind, lack of soil, etc.

SEPAL – One of the segments of the calyx, usually leaf-like; sometimes, as in most orchids, petal-like.

SERRATE – Saw-toothed, with the teeth pointing forward.

SESSILE – Stemless, as in leaves or flowers arising directly from a main stem.

SHRUB – A woody plant that remains low, usually with more than one trunk. Not a precise descriptive term.

SPECIES (singular and plural) – The basic unit of classification of living things. Species are grouped into genera. The scientific name is composed of two words: the genus name, identifying the larger group, followed by the species name, identifying the particular kind. The genus *Ficus,* for example, the figs, is an exceptionally large genus, containing about 800 species. Some of the more familiar are *Ficus carica,* the edible fig; *Ficus elastica,* the rubber tree; *Ficus benghalensis,* the banyan; *Ficus benjamina,* the weeping fig. Species may be further divided into subspecies, varieties and forms, in descending order of classification.

SPIKE – Usually an unbranched elongated flower stalk with stemless flowers.

SPINE – A sharp hard protrusion; usually a modified leaf. Compare thorn.

STAMEN – The pollen producing organ in a flower, usually made up of a filament and an anther.

STIPULE – A small appendage at the bases of the leaf stalks on some plants, usually occurring in pairs, extremely variable in form.

SUCCULENT – Thickened, juicy; a plant that stores water in fleshy parts.

THORN – A sharp projection from the stem of a plant, usually a modified twig. Compare spine.

TREE – A large woody plant, usually with a single trunk.

TUBER – A modified underground stem, much thickened and fleshy, as in potatoes.

VEIN – A bundle of externally visible conducting and supporting tissue in a leaf or other plant part.

WHORL – A group of three or more leaves or other parts at the same node.

Selected References

Acevedo-Rodriquez, Pedro. *The Flora of St. John U.S. Virgin Islands.* The New York Botanical Garden, Bronx, NY, 1996

Acevedo-Rodriquez, Pedro & Roy O. Woodbury. *Los Bejucos de Puerto Rico. Vol. 1,* U.S. Forest Service General Technical Report. SO-58:1–331 (1985).

Ackerman, James D.. *The Orchids of Puerto Rico and the Virgin Islands.* Editorial de la Universidad de Puerto Rico, Rio Piedras, PR, 1992.

Arvigo, Rosita & Michael Balick. *Rainforest Remedies—One Hundred Healing Herbs of Belize.* Lotus Press, Twin Lakes, WI, 1993.

Britton, Nathaniel Lord & Percy Wilson. *Botany of Puerto Rico and the Virgin Islands.* Scientific Survey of Puerto Rico and the Virgin Islands, New York Academy of Sciences, New York, 1923–1926.

Honychurch, Penelope N. *Caribbean Wild Plants and Their Uses,* Macmillan Caribbean, London and Oxford, 1980.

Howard, Richard A. *Flora of the Lesser Antilles.* Arnold Arboretum of Harvard University, Jamaica Plain, MA, 1974–1989.

Kemp, Bernard A. & Guy H. Benjamin. *The Economic Way of Life of East End, St. John.* Unpublished manuscript. St. John VI, 1989–2003

Liogier, Henri A. *Plantas Medicinales de Puerto Rico y del Caribe.* Iberoamericana de Ediciones. San Juan, PR, 1990.

Little, Elbert L. Jr. & Frank H. Wadsworth. *Common Trees of Puerto Rico and the Virgin Islands.* Agriculture Handbook No. 249, US Forest Service, Washington, DC, 1964.

Little, Elbert l. Jr. & Roy O. Woodbury. *Rare and Endemic Trees of Puerto Rico and the Virgin Islands.* U.S.D.A. Conservation Research Report 27: 1–26, 1980.

Little, Elbert L. Jr. & Roy O. Woodbury & Frank H. Wadsworth. *Trees of Puerto Rico and the Virgin Islands Vol. 2.* Agriculture Handbook No. 449, U.S. Forest Service, Washington, DC,. 1974

Nellis, David W. *Poisonous Plants and Animals of South Florida and the Caribbean.* Pineapple Press, Sarasota, FL, 1997.

Nellis, David W. *Seashore Plants of South Florida and the Caribbean,* Pineapple Press, Sarasota, FL, 1994.

Oldendorp, C. G. A. *History of the Mission of the Evangelical Brethren on the Caribbean Islands of St. Thomas, St. Croix and St. John.* 1777. Translated from the German in 1987 by A.R Highfield & V. Barac. Karoma Publishers, Ann Arbor, MI.

Thomas, Toni A. *Traditional Medicinal Plants of St. Croix, St. Thomas and St. John.* University of the Virgin Islands, St. Thomas and St. Croix, VI, 1997.

Index To Common and Scientific Names

Addendum: Endemic Trees & Plants

Trees:

Cordia rickseckeri, 20
Reynosia guama, 34

Shrubs:

Eugenia sessiflora, 43
Machonia woodburyana, 50, 51
Pictetia aculeata, 54
Piptocoma antillansa, 55
Rondeletia pilosa, 57
Scolosanthus versicolor, 59

Succulents

Agave missionum, 68